Auckland in 3 Days Travel Guide

(https://pixabay.com/en/auckland-new-zealand-city-tower-927242/)

Welcome to this travel guide to Auckland! Many visitors to New Zealand do not plan enough time to explore Auckland, instead opting to visit the natural beauty of the South Island. Nevertheless, Auckland is a worthwhile destination in its own right. Even if you just want a few days to relax and get over jet lag, Auckland has something to offer all kinds of tourists. From nightlife and dining to gorgeous beaches and volcano hikes, Auckland is full of surprises. New Zealand's largest city can easily compete with the more famous Australian cities, and should not be overlooked on your trip to Aotearoa.

We have written this guide with the help of local experts and travel bloggers who have visited the city. Auckland is classed as a supercity due to its nature as a conglomeration of four cities - Auckland City, Waitakere City, North Shore City, and Manukau City. It is home to one-third of the population of New Zealand, meaning there is a lot to do across the four districts. We've kept this in mind when writing this guide, allowing you to explore the city at an easy pace. Though we have stuck to Auckland City and North Shore City in the 3-day itinerary, there is plenty to explore in the other regions so we have included a small section about these regions if you want to venture a little further out.

There is also some information about tours available from Auckland CBD (Central Business District) if you want to explore a little further. We've restricted these to the Auckland, Northland, and Waikato regions, as these are easily accessible and are more suitable for day trips.

All of the maps in this guide can also be accessed through Google Maps with the attached link. We suggest saving them to your phone before you arrive to make the trip a little bit easier.
We hope you enjoy your trip to Auckland and leave the city happy that you didn't miss it out. Thank you for choosing a Guidora Guide!

Table of Contents

1. Introduction to Auckland

Brief overview of the city

Auckland is a city located on the North Island of New Zealand. It is the largest and most populous city in the country, with a population of over 1.6 million people. Auckland is known for its stunning natural beauty, vibrant cultural scene, and diverse range of activities and attractions.

The city is built on a narrow isthmus between two harbors, the Waitemata and the Manukau. The Waitemata Harbor is the more prominent of the two, and it is often referred to as the "City of Sails" due to the large number of boats and yachts that can be seen in its waters. The city is also surrounded by a number of volcanoes, which give it a unique landscape and provide visitors with some excellent hiking opportunities.

One of the things that makes Auckland so appealing to visitors is its mild and pleasant climate. The city enjoys warm summers and mild winters, making it an ideal destination for those who want to escape the colder temperatures of other parts of the world. The summer months are the most popular time to visit Auckland, as the city comes alive with outdoor events and festivals.

In terms of culture, Auckland has a rich and diverse history. The city was first settled by the Maori people, who named the area Tamaki Makaurau, which means "Tamaki of a hundred lovers." The first European settlers arrived in the early 19th century, and since then the city has grown and developed into a multicultural hub of activity.

Today, Auckland is a bustling metropolis that is home to a wide range of people from different backgrounds and cultures. The city is known for its excellent food scene, with a wide range of restaurants and cafes serving up everything from traditional Maori cuisine to international favorites. The city also boasts a thriving arts scene, with numerous galleries, theaters, and music venues showcasing the best of local and international talent.

For those who love the outdoors, Auckland is a paradise. The city is surrounded by a number of stunning natural attractions, including the Waitakere Ranges and the Hauraki Gulf Islands. Visitors can go hiking, surfing, swimming, or simply enjoy a relaxing day at one of the many beautiful beaches.

In terms of getting around, Auckland has an excellent public transportation system, with buses, trains, and ferries connecting the city to its surrounding areas. The city is also very pedestrian and bike-friendly, with a number of dedicated paths and routes that make it easy to explore the city on foot or by bike.

Overall, Auckland is a fantastic destination for anyone looking to experience the best of New Zealand's natural beauty, culture, and cuisine. Whether you're interested in hiking through the rugged wilderness or taking in a show at the theater, Auckland has something for everyone.

History of Auckland

The history of Auckland dates back to the arrival of the Maori people in the area over 800 years ago. The Maori named the area Tamaki Makaurau, which means "Tamaki of a hundred lovers," after a local chief who had many wives. The Maori people were skilled navigators and fishermen, and they established thriving communities along the coast.

The first Europeans arrived in the area in the early 19th century, led by British explorer Captain James Cook. Cook sailed into the Waitemata Harbor in 1769, but it wasn't until the 1830s that Europeans began to settle in the area. In 1840, the Treaty of Waitangi was signed, which established British sovereignty over New Zealand and gave the Maori people certain rights and protections.

The settlement of Auckland grew rapidly in the mid-19th century, as more and more Europeans arrived in the area. The city was initially named after the Earl of Auckland, who was the Governor-General of India at the time. Auckland became the capital of New Zealand in 1841, but this was only temporary, and the capital was later moved to Wellington.

During the 1860s, Auckland became an important center for trade and commerce, thanks to its strategic location on the Waitemata Harbor. The city grew rapidly during this time, with the construction of numerous buildings and infrastructure projects. The first railway in New Zealand was built between Auckland and the nearby town of Onehunga in 1873, further cementing Auckland's status as a major transport hub.

In the early 20th century, Auckland continued to grow and develop, as new suburbs were established and the city's infrastructure was expanded. The construction of the Auckland Harbour Bridge in 1959 was a major milestone in the city's history, as it connected Auckland's two harbors and made it easier for people and goods to move around the city.

Throughout its history, Auckland has been influenced by a number of different cultures and communities. The Maori people have played an important role in the city's history and culture, and their traditions and customs continue to be celebrated today. European settlers have also left their mark on the city, particularly in terms of architecture and urban planning.

In recent years, Auckland has become a multicultural hub of activity, with people from all over the world coming to live and work in the city. The city's diverse population has led to a vibrant arts and cultural scene, with numerous festivals, events, and exhibitions taking place throughout the year. Today, Auckland is the largest and most populous city in New Zealand, with a population of over 1.6 million people. The city continues to grow and develop, with new infrastructure projects and developments planned for the future. Despite its rapid growth, however, Auckland has managed to retain its unique character and charm, making it a fascinating destination for visitors from all over the world.

Geography and climate of Auckland

Auckland's geography and climate play a significant role in the city's appeal and attractions. The city is located on the North Island of New Zealand, and it covers an area of approximately 1,086 square kilometers. Auckland is situated on a narrow isthmus between two harbors, the Waitemata and the Manukau. The Waitemata Harbor is the more prominent of the two, and it is often referred to as the "City of Sails" due to the large number of boats and yachts that can be seen in its waters.

Auckland's landscape is dominated by a number of volcanoes, which give the city a unique appearance and provide visitors with some excellent hiking opportunities. The most prominent of these volcanoes is Mount Eden, which stands at a height of 196 meters and offers stunning views of the city and its surroundings.

The city's geography also includes a number of beautiful beaches, parks, and natural reserves. Some of the most popular beaches in Auckland include Mission Bay, Takapuna Beach, and Piha Beach. These beaches offer visitors a chance to swim, surf, and relax in the sun, and they are also popular spots for picnics and barbecues.

In terms of climate, Auckland enjoys a mild and pleasant climate throughout the year. The city experiences warm summers and mild winters, with temperatures ranging from 20°C to 30°C in the summer months and 10°C to 15°C in the winter months. The average temperature in Auckland is around 15°C, making it an ideal destination for those who want to escape the colder temperatures of other parts of the world.

Auckland also experiences a moderate amount of rainfall throughout the year, with the wettest months being between June and September. However, the rain is usually brief and light, and it rarely interferes with outdoor activities or travel plans.

One of the unique features of Auckland's climate is its "microclimates," which are caused by the city's varied geography. The western parts of the city tend to be wetter and cooler than the eastern parts, which are more sheltered and warmer. The city's volcanoes also have a significant impact on the local climate, with temperatures on the summit of Mount Eden often being several degrees cooler than at sea level.

Overall, Auckland's geography and climate make it a beautiful and appealing destination for visitors from all over the world. Whether you're interested in hiking through the rugged wilderness, relaxing on a beautiful beach, or exploring the city's vibrant cultural scene, Auckland has something to offer everyone.

Useful Information

Official Language: New Zealand has three official languages - English, Māori, and New Zealand Sign Language. English is the main language used in the country, however, locals like to incorporate Māori words into everyday speech, and learning some basic terms will be very appreciated by the indigenous population. There are also some unique Kiwi slang terms used in New Zealand English. We have included some regularly used Māori terms and NZ slang words in the useful phrases section.

Time Zone: GMT/UTC +12. New Zealand also observes Daylight Savings Time - keep in mind that as it is in the Southern Hemisphere, the clocks go forward one hour from October to April.

Metric System: Kilograms, centimetres and celsius.

Entry Requirements: Visitors to New Zealand must have a valid passport and may also need a visa, depending on their country of origin. Check with the New Zealand embassy or consulate in your home country to determine what entry requirements apply to you.

Currency: The currency in New Zealand is the New Zealand dollar (NZD). ATMs are widely available throughout the city, and major credit cards are widely accepted.

Language: English is the official language of New Zealand, and is spoken by the majority of the population. Maori is also an official language and is widely spoken throughout the country.

Transportation: Auckland has a range of transportation options, including buses, trains, ferries, and taxis. The Auckland Transport website provides information on routes, schedules, and fares, as well as a handy journey planner to help you get around the city.

Weather: Auckland has a temperate climate, with mild winters and warm summers. Be sure to pack appropriate clothing for the time of year, and be prepared for occasional rain showers.

Safety: Auckland is generally a safe city for visitors, but it's always a good idea to take basic precautions such as keeping an eye on your belongings and avoiding isolated areas at night.

Electricity: New Zealand operates on 230-240 volts, 50Hz AC power, with three-pin power outlets. If you're traveling from a country with a different voltage, you may need a voltage converter and plug adapter.

Emergency Numbers: Police, Fire, and Ambulance: 111

Key Embassies in Auckland:
- United States Embassy: 29 Fitzherbert Terrace, Thorndon, Wellington 6011. Phone: +64 4 462 6000. Website: https://nz.usembassy.gov/
- British High Commission: 44 Hill Street, Thorndon, Wellington 6011. Phone: +64 4 924 2888. Website: https://www.gov.uk/world/organisations/british-high-commission-wellington
- Australian High Commission: 72-76 Hobson Street, Thorndon, Wellington 6011. Phone: +64 4 473 6411. Website: https://www.newzealand.embassy.gov.au/wltn/home.html
- Canadian High Commission: 125 The Terrace, Wellington 6011. Phone: +64 4 473 9577. Website: https://www.canadainternational.gc.ca/new_zealand-nouvelle_zelande/index.aspx?lang=eng

In case of emergency, visitors can also contact their country's embassy or consulate in New Zealand for assistance.

It's a good idea to keep these numbers and addresses on hand during your trip, in case of any unexpected situations that may arise.

Tipping: Though tipping is not expected in New Zealand, it is very appreciated. For restaurants, tip around 15-20% if you enjoyed the service. New Zealanders take their coffee very seriously, so it is customary to give your barista an extra dollar tip if you enjoyed the coffee. For cabs, it is never expected to tip, but drivers will not be offended if you choose to do so.

Cost of living: The cost of living in New Zealand is high, and Auckland is generally pricier than the rest of the country. Cost of living in the city is roughly comparable with major Australian cities and considerably more than most North American and European countries.

- Meal in an inexpensive restaurant: NZ$12-18
- Three-course meal in a mid-range restaurant: NZ$85
- 0.33 liters of water: NZ$2.50
- Local transport (one way): NZ$4
- Cost of a bottle of beer in a bar: NZ$9-10
- Double room in an average hotel: NZ$175

Average internet speed: 61.21mbps

Credit cards: Most places in New Zealand will accept credit cards as the country aims to go cashless. There are two types of card - EFTPOS (debit card) and credit cards. If you are using a foreign debit card you will still need to use the "credit" button on card machines and ATMs. Most major credit cards are accepted - with even American Express being widely used.

Dial code: +64

Health Insurance: New Zealand has a universal healthcare system, however, this is reserved for residents and non-resident taxpayers. We suggest purchasing insurance before you go, however in the case of emergencies you will not be turned away and prices are still considerably lower than in the US. If you are visiting from the UK or Australia, New Zealand has a reciprocal healthcare agreement meaning you will pay the same rate as locals.

Visa Requirements: Visa requirements differ from country to country. All visitors - even those visa-free - will need to register for travel authorization online before arrival and fill out a customs form during the flight.

Citizens of the UK can visit visa-free for up to six months, whilst most other European and North American nations can visit for up to three months. Australians can remain in New Zealand indefinitely, and have full employment and education rights.

New Zealand also has the most working holiday visa agreements with other countries, so this is worth checking if you are under 30 and want to stay for up to a year (or two years if you are from the UK).

2.Getting to Auckland

Getting to Auckland is relatively easy, as the city is a major transport hub and is well-connected to other parts of New Zealand and the world. Visitors can reach Auckland by air, road, or sea, with a number of options available for each mode of transportation. The city is home to Auckland Airport, which is the largest and busiest airport in New Zealand, and it is serviced by a number of international and domestic airlines. Public transportation in Auckland is also well-developed, with buses, trains, and ferries connecting the city to its surrounding areas. Whether you're coming from across the world or from a nearby town, getting to Auckland is a breeze.

Air travel to Auckland

Air travel is one of the most popular ways to get to Auckland, as the city is serviced by Auckland Airport, which is the largest and busiest airport in New Zealand. The airport is located approximately 21 kilometers from the city center and is well-connected to other parts of the city and surrounding areas.

Auckland Airport serves as a hub for Air New Zealand, which operates a number of international and domestic flights from the airport. In addition, the airport is also serviced by a number of other international and domestic airlines, including Qantas, Emirates, and Jetstar.

International flights to Auckland arrive from a number of destinations around the world, including Australia, Asia, Europe, and North America. Direct flights are available from a number of cities, including Los Angeles, San Francisco, Vancouver, Singapore, Sydney, and Melbourne.

Domestic flights to Auckland are also widely available, with connections to other major cities in New Zealand, including Wellington, Christchurch, and Queenstown. Domestic flights are operated by Air New Zealand, Jetstar, and other regional airlines.

Getting to and from Auckland Airport is easy, with a number of public transportation options available. The airport is served by a dedicated bus service, called the Airbus Express, which provides regular connections to the city center and other parts of Auckland. In addition, there are a number of taxi and shuttle services available, which can be pre-booked or hired upon arrival at the airport.

Overall, air travel is a convenient and efficient way to get to Auckland, with a number of international and domestic flights available from Auckland Airport. Whether you're traveling from across the world or from a nearby city, getting to Auckland by air is a breeze.

Public transportation options in Auckland

Public transportation in Auckland is well-developed and provides visitors with a convenient and cost-effective way to get around the city and its surrounding areas. There are several options for public transportation in Auckland, including buses, trains, and ferries.

Buses are the most common form of public transportation in Auckland, with a network of over 200 bus routes connecting the city to its suburbs and neighboring towns. The buses are operated by several companies, including Auckland Transport and NZ Bus, and are known for being safe, reliable, and comfortable. The fares for buses in Auckland vary depending on the route and the distance traveled, but generally range from NZD $1.50 to NZD $6.00 for a one-way trip.

Trains are another popular form of public transportation in Auckland, with several train lines connecting the city to its suburbs and neighboring towns. The trains are operated by Transdev Auckland and are known for being fast, efficient, and comfortable. The fares for trains in Auckland vary depending on the route and the distance traveled, but generally range from NZD $2.20 to NZD $8.00 for a one-way trip.

Ferries are also an option for public transportation in Auckland, with several ferry services connecting the city to its surrounding islands and coastal towns. The ferries are operated by Fullers and SeaLink and provide a scenic and enjoyable way to explore the city and its surroundings. The fares for ferries in Auckland vary depending on the route and the distance traveled, but generally range from NZD $7.50 to NZD $15.00 for a one-way trip. Auckland Transport is the main organization responsible for public transportation in Auckland, and they provide a wealth of information and resources for visitors. Their website, www.at.govt.nz, is a useful resource for planning your travel around the city and finding information on fares, routes, and schedules. The website also offers a range of useful tools, such as a journey planner and a real-time bus tracker, which can help you navigate the city more easily.

In addition to traditional public transportation options, visitors to Auckland can also make use of **ride-hailing services** such as **Uber** and **Ola**. These services are widely available in Auckland and can be a convenient and affordable way to get around the city. Taxi services are also available, although they tend to be more expensive than other forms of public transportation.
Overall, public transportation in Auckland is an excellent option for visitors who want to explore the city and its surroundings without the hassle and expense of renting a car.

Navigating Auckland: maps and apps

Navigating Auckland is relatively easy, with well-marked streets and signage. However, having a map or a GPS device is helpful, especially when exploring new areas. Free city maps are available at tourist information centers and many hotels.
Mobile apps can be invaluable for navigating Auckland's public transportation system, finding nearby attractions, and planning your daily itinerary. Some useful apps for navigating Auckland include:

- AT Mobile: Official app for Auckland Transport, providing information on bus, train, and ferry timetables, route planning, and live updates.
- Google Maps: Offers detailed maps, directions, and real-time traffic information for driving, walking, and public transport.
- Moovit: Provides real-time public transit information, including arrival times and service alerts, as well as step-by-step navigation.
- Neat Places: Offers curated recommendations for local attractions, dining, shopping, and events, based on your location and preferences.

Driving to Auckland

Driving to Auckland is a popular option for visitors who want to explore the city and its surroundings at their own pace. The city is well-connected to other parts of New Zealand by a network of highways and motorways, and driving to Auckland can be a scenic and enjoyable experience.

If you are driving to Auckland from another part of New Zealand, there are several highways and motorways that connect the city to other major cities and towns. The Northern Motorway connects Auckland to the Northland region, while the Southern Motorway connects the city to Hamilton and the Waikato region. The Western Motorway provides access to the west coast of Auckland and the Waitakere Ranges.

If you are driving to Auckland from outside of New Zealand, you will need to hire a car or bring your own vehicle. The process of hiring a car in Auckland is straightforward, with several major rental car companies operating in the city, including Hertz, Avis, and Budget. Prices for rental cars vary depending on the type of vehicle and the duration of the rental, but generally range from NZD $50 to NZD $150 per day.

When driving in Auckland, it is important to be aware of the city's traffic conditions and road rules. Traffic in Auckland can be heavy during peak hours, particularly on the motorways and main arterial routes. It is also important to pay attention to the speed limits, which vary depending on the area and the type of road. The speed limit in urban areas is generally 50 km/h, while on the motorways it is 100 km/h.

Parking in Auckland can be a challenge, particularly in the city center and other busy areas. There are several public parking lots available throughout the city, as well as metered parking on the streets. It is important to be aware of parking restrictions, as fines can be issued for parking in prohibited areas or exceeding the time limit.

How to get from the airport to Auckland CBD

The airport is located 25km south of the CBD in Manukau City. It is well connected to the city and you have three main options - the Airbus, regular bus, and train, shuttle or taxi.

The Airbus stop is located just outside the terminal. It connects to both the international and domestic terminal, and goes directly to Auckland CBD, with many stops across central Auckland. You can purchase tickets in advance online, which will save you a little bit of money, or buy them from the clerk next to the bus stop. The bus is air-conditioned and has WiFi, and will get you to the CBD in 30 minutes if traffic is clear. Do keep in mind, however, that Auckland traffic is famously bad and it will likely take you much longer - especially during peak hours.

You can also opt to take the 380 bus from the airport to Papatoetoe (pronounced pah-pah-toi-toi) Station. You can then get the train from there straight to Britomart Station in the CBD. This is only marginally cheaper and quicker, however, it is a good option if you want to avoid excessive traffic during peak hours.

Shuttles can be arranged via your hotel, online or at the airport kiosks. If you are booking at the airport, all of the shuttle services are located within the terminal close to the car rental kiosks. If you are staying outside of the city center, this is a better option than public transport. Most drivers will wait a little bit before departing in case any other passengers heading in the same direction arrive, however, there are regulations in place to minimize how long they can wait. It can be a little expensive but is still considerably cheaper than a taxi.

If you want to splash out on a taxi, most of them run a flat rate and therefore prices are not influenced by how bad the traffic is. At peak times, this option is no quicker than the bus however can be a little bit more comfortable and will take you directly to any destination within the city. The price from the airport to the CBD varies between $50-100, so we suggest negotiating a set price before you depart. Uber charges a flat rate of $70, whilst Zoomy (the main rival to Uber in Auckland) charges from $40-70 depending on the time of day.

3.Accommodation in Auckland

Auckland offers a wide range of accommodation options for visitors, from luxury hotels to budget-friendly hostels and everything in between. Whether you're looking for a chic boutique hotel in the heart of the city, a cozy bed and breakfast in a quiet suburb, or a hostel that caters to backpackers and budget-conscious travelers, Auckland has something to suit every taste and budget. With a wealth of options available, finding the perfect place to stay in Auckland can be a daunting task, but with some careful research and planning, you can find a comfortable and convenient home away from home during your visit to this vibrant city.

Types of accommodation in Auckland

Auckland offers a wide range of accommodation options to suit every taste and budget. Whether you're looking for a luxury hotel, a cozy bed and breakfast, or a budget-friendly hostel, you're sure to find something that fits your needs in this vibrant city. Here are some of the most popular types of accommodation in Auckland:

- Hotels: Auckland is home to a wide range of hotels, from luxurious five-star properties to more affordable options. Many of the city's hotels are located in the central business district, providing easy access to the city's attractions, restaurants, and shops.
- Bed and Breakfasts: For those seeking a more intimate and personalized experience, bed and breakfasts are a great option. Auckland has a number of charming bed and breakfasts located in quiet neighborhoods, offering comfortable accommodations and personalized service.
- Apartments and Vacation Rentals: If you're planning a longer stay in Auckland, renting an apartment or vacation rental can be a great option. There are a number of rental properties available throughout the city, ranging from small studios to large family-friendly apartments.

- Hostels: Auckland has a number of hostels catering to backpackers and budget-conscious travelers. Hostels offer affordable accommodation and often have a lively and social atmosphere, making them a great option for solo travelers and groups.
- Campgrounds and Holiday Parks: For those who love the great outdoors, Auckland has several campgrounds and holiday parks located throughout the city and its surrounding areas. These parks offer a range of accommodation options, from basic tent sites to fully-equipped cabins.

Whether you're looking for luxury or budget-friendly accommodation, Auckland has something to suit every taste and budget. With a wealth of options available, it's easy to find the perfect place to stay during your visit to this exciting city.

Best areas to stay in Auckland

Auckland offers a variety of neighborhoods and areas to stay in, each with its own unique charm and attractions. Here are some of the best areas to stay in Auckland, along with their pros and cons and things to do in the area:

Central Business District (CBD): The CBD is the heart of Auckland and is home to many of the city's best restaurants, shops, and attractions. The area is well-connected to public transportation, making it easy to explore other parts of the city. However, the CBD can be quite busy and noisy, particularly during peak hours. Some of the top attractions in the CBD include the Sky Tower, the Auckland Art Gallery, and the Auckland War Memorial Museum.

Ponsonby: Ponsonby is a trendy neighborhood located just west of the CBD. The area is known for its hip cafes, boutiques, and bars, and has a lively and cosmopolitan atmosphere. However, accommodation in Ponsonby can be more expensive than other areas of Auckland. Some of the top attractions in Ponsonby include the Ponsonby Central market, the Westhaven Marina, and the Victoria Park Market.

Parnell: Parnell is a historic neighborhood located just east of the CBD. The area is home to many beautiful old buildings, boutique shops, and charming cafes. Accommodation in Parnell tends to be more expensive than other areas, but the neighborhood's charm and convenient location make it a popular choice for visitors. Some of the top attractions in Parnell include the Parnell Rose Gardens, the Auckland Domain, and the Parnell Village Farmers' Market.

Viaduct Harbour: Viaduct Harbour is a popular area located on the waterfront in the CBD. The area is known for its stunning views, trendy bars, and upscale restaurants. However, accommodation in Viaduct Harbour can be expensive, and the area can be quite crowded during peak tourist season. Some of the top attractions in Viaduct Harbour include the Auckland Fish Market, the Maritime Museum, and the Auckland Harbour Bridge.

Devonport: Devonport is a charming seaside suburb located just across the harbor from the CBD. The area is known for its beautiful beaches, historic architecture, and peaceful atmosphere. Accommodation in Devonport tends to be more affordable than other areas of Auckland, and the neighborhood's proximity to the CBD makes it a convenient option for visitors. Some of the top attractions in Devonport include the Devonport Naval Base, the Devonport Craft Market, and the North Head Historic Reserve.

Overall, Auckland offers a wide range of neighborhoods and areas to stay in, each with its own unique attractions and charm. By considering your budget, interests, and preferred location, you can find the perfect area to stay during your visit to this vibrant and exciting city.

Recommended hotels and hostels in Auckland

SkyCity Grand Hotel - Located in the heart of Auckland's CBD, the SkyCity Grand Hotel is a luxurious five-star hotel with stunning views of the city skyline. The hotel features a range of amenities, including an indoor pool, spa, and fitness center. However, the SkyCity Grand Hotel can be quite expensive, with rooms starting at around NZD $250 per night. Website: https://www.skycityauckland.co.nz/hotels/skycity-grand/; Physical Address: 90 Federal Street, Auckland, New Zealand; Phone: +64 9-363 6000

The Sebel Auckland Viaduct Harbour - This upscale hotel is located in the heart of Auckland's Viaduct Harbour area and offers stunning views of the harbor and city skyline. The hotel features spacious rooms, a fitness center, and an outdoor pool. However, prices at The Sebel Auckland Viaduct Harbour can be quite high, with rooms starting at around NZD $300 per night. Website: https://www.thesebel.com/hotel-listings/the-sebel-auckland-viaduct-harbour/; Physical Address: 85-89 Customs Street West, Auckland, New Zealand; Phone: +64 9-978 4000

Nomads Auckland Backpackers - For budget-conscious travelers, Nomads Auckland Backpackers is a popular option. This centrally located hostel offers clean and comfortable dormitory-style accommodations, as well as private rooms. The hostel features a communal kitchen, lounge area, and laundry facilities. However, some guests have reported that the hostel can be noisy and crowded. Prices at Nomads Auckland Backpackers start at around NZD $20 per night. Website: https://nomadsworld.com/hostels/new-zealand/nomads-auckland-backpackers/; Address: 16-20 Fort Street, Auckland, New Zealand; Phone: +64 9-300 9999

Haka Lodge Auckland - This modern and stylish hostel is located in Auckland's central business district and offers a range of accommodations, including private rooms and dormitory-style rooms. The hostel features a communal kitchen, lounge area, and outdoor terrace. Prices at Haka Lodge Auckland start at around NZD $35 per night. However, some guests have reported that the hostel can be noisy at times. Website: https://hakalodge.com/hostels/new-zealand-hostels/haka-lodge-auckland/; Address: 373 Karangahape Road, Auckland, New Zealand; Phone: +64 9-282 1220

Overall, Auckland offers a variety of accommodations to suit every budget and preference. By considering your needs and preferences, you can find the perfect place to stay during your visit to this exciting and vibrant city.

Unique stays: boutique hotels, bed and breakfasts, and eco-friendly lodgings

1. Mollies Boutique Hotel
Website: https://www.mollies.co.nz/ Description: Mollies Boutique Hotel is a luxurious, intimate hotel set in a Victorian villa in the trendy suburb of Ponsonby. The hotel offers 15 elegantly designed suites, each with its own distinct character and charm. Guests can enjoy fine dining at the on-site restaurant, relax in the serene garden, or indulge in a spa treatment. Average price: NZD 300-600 per night

2. City Garden Lodge (Bed and Breakfast)
Website: http://www.citygardenlodge.co.nz/ Description: City Garden Lodge is a charming bed and breakfast located in a historic Edwardian-style house in the Parnell neighborhood. The lodge offers a range of comfortable and affordable private rooms, along with a beautiful garden, a cozy lounge area, and a well-equipped communal kitchen. Average price: NZD 70-120 per night

3. The Great Ponsonby Arthotel (Bed and Breakfast)
Website: https://www.greatpons.co.nz/ Description: The Great Ponsonby Arthotel is a vibrant bed and breakfast set in a colorful villa in the heart of

Ponsonby. Each of the 11 rooms is individually decorated with eclectic artwork, showcasing New Zealand's art scene. Guests can enjoy a delicious home-cooked breakfast, relax in the tranquil garden, or explore the nearby cafes and galleries. Average price: NZD 180-300 per night

4.   Earthsong Lodge (Eco-Friendly Lodge)
Website: https://www.earthsonglodge.co.nz/ Description: Earthsong Lodge an award-winning eco-friendly lodge located on Great Barrier Island, a shor flight or ferry ride from Auckland. The lodge offers luxurious accommodations in a serene natural setting, with stunning views of the ocean and native bush. Guests can enjoy fine dining with locally sourced ingredients, guided nature walks, and a range of activities such as kayaking, fishing, and stargazing. Average price: NZD 700-1200 per night

Please note that these prices are approximate and may vary depending on the season, room type, and availability. It is recommended to check the respective websites or contact the properties for the most up-to-date pricing and availability information.

4.Things to do in Auckland

Auckland is a vibrant and exciting city with a wealth of attractions and activities to explore. From stunning natural landscapes and beautiful beaches to world-class museums and cultural events, Auckland offers something for everyone. Whether you're interested in outdoor adventures, art and culture, or simply soaking up the city's lively atmosphere, Auckland has plenty to offer. In this section, we'll explore some of the top things to do in Auckland, including must-see attractions, hidden gems, and insider tips for making the most of your visit to this amazing city.

Top tourist attractions in Auckland

Auckland is home to a wealth of tourist attractions, from stunning natural landscapes and beautiful beaches to world-class museums and cultural events. Whether you're visiting Auckland for the first time or returning for another trip, there are plenty of must-see attractions that you won't want to miss. Here are some of the top tourist attractions in Auckland:

- **Sky Tower:** The Sky Tower is one of Auckland's most iconic landmarks, offering stunning views of the city and its surroundings. At 328 meters tall, the tower is the tallest freestanding structure in the Southern Hemisphere and is home to several observation decks, a revolving restaurant, and a bungee jumping platform. Visitors can take a lift to the top of the tower for panoramic views of the city and the harbor below.
- **Auckland Harbour Bridge:** The Auckland Harbour Bridge is another iconic landmark in the city and offers stunning views of the harbor and city skyline. Visitors can walk or cycle across the bridge, take a guided tour, or even bungee jump from the bridge's highest point. The bridge also features a unique light show at night, with thousands of LED lights illuminating the structure.
- **Auckland War Memorial Museum:** The Auckland War Memorial Museum is one of the city's top cultural attractions, offering an insight

into New Zealand's history and culture. The museum features a range of exhibits, including displays on Maori culture, New Zealand's involvement in World War I and II, and natural history. The museum is also home to a stunning collection of Maori artifacts, including carvings, textiles, and weapons.

- **Waiheke Island:** Waiheke Island is a beautiful island located just off the coast of Auckland and is known for its stunning beaches, vineyards, and art galleries. Visitors can take a ferry from Auckland to Waiheke Island and spend the day exploring the island's many attractions, including the stunning Onetangi Beach, the award-winning Mudbrick Vineyard, and the Waiheke Island Art Gallery.
- **Auckland Zoo:** The Auckland Zoo is home to a wide range of exotic animals, including elephants, lions, and giraffes. The zoo features several themed exhibits, including the African Savannah, the Tropical Rainforest, and the New Zealand Birds and Reptiles exhibit. Visitors can also take part in animal encounters and behind-the-scenes tours to learn more about the zoo's inhabitants.
- **Rangitoto Island:** Rangitoto Island is a volcanic island located in the Hauraki Gulf and is home to some of Auckland's most stunning natural scenery. Visitors can take a ferry to the island and hike to the summit of the volcano for panoramic views of the city and the surrounding islands. The island is also home to several beaches, including the stunning Blackpool Beach.
- **Auckland Domain:** The Auckland Domain is a large park located in the heart of the city and is home to several attractions, including the Auckland War Memorial Museum and the Wintergardens. The park also features several walking trails, picnic areas, and stunning views of the city skyline.

Overall, Auckland offers a wealth of tourist attractions and activities to explore. Whether you're interested in natural scenery, cultural attractions, or adventure activities, there's something for everyone in this vibrant and exciting city. By visiting these top tourist attractions in Auckland, you'll gain a deeper understanding of the city's history and culture, while also experiencing some of its most stunning natural scenery and exciting activities.

Unique Experiences

Auckland is a city full of unique experiences that are sure to leave a lasting impression on visitors. From the natural wonders to the cultural attractions, there is no shortage of interesting things to see and do in this vibrant city. Here are some of the most unique experiences to have in Auckland:

- **Climb the Auckland Harbour Bridge** - Take a guided climb up the Auckland Harbour Bridge for an unforgettable view of the city skyline and Waitemata Harbour. The climb includes a safety briefing and all necessary equipment, and visitors can choose from day or night climbs.
- **Visit a glowworm cave** - Take a short drive from Auckland to the Waitomo Caves, where you can witness thousands of tiny glowworms illuminating the darkness. Take a guided tour to learn about the history and geology of the caves while exploring the subterranean wonders.
- **Visit the Auckland War Memorial Museum** - The Auckland War Memorial Museum is a must-visit for history buffs, with exhibits covering New Zealand's military history and the country's natural and cultural heritage. Visitors can also experience a traditional Maori cultural performance.
- **SkyJump off the Sky Tower** - The Sky Tower is an iconic part of the Auckland skyline, and visitors can take their experience to the next level with a SkyJump. This thrilling activity involves jumping off the tower while attached to a wire, providing a unique and exhilarating view of the city below.
- **Go wine tasting on Waiheke Island** - A short ferry ride from Auckland, Waiheke Island is home to some of New Zealand's best vineyards and wineries. Take a tour and taste some of the country's finest wines while enjoying the island's stunning scenery.
- **Visit the Auckland Art Gallery** - The Auckland Art Gallery is home to one of the largest and most comprehensive collections of art in New

Zealand, with works ranging from classic to contemporary. Visitors can also enjoy regular special exhibitions and events.

- **Go sailing on the Waitemata Harbour** - Auckland is known as the "City of Sails" due to its love of sailing, and visitors can experience this passion firsthand by taking a sailing tour of the Waitemata Harbour. This is a great way to see the city from a unique perspective while enjoying the sea breeze.

These unique experiences are just a few of the many things to see and do in Auckland. Whether you're interested in adventure, culture, or relaxation, Auckland has something to offer for every type of traveler.

Family-friendly attractions and activities in Auckland

1. Auckland Zoo

Website: https://www.aucklandzoo.co.nz/ Description: Auckland Zoo is home to over 1400 animals representing 135 different species, making it a perfect day out for families. The zoo offers interactive experiences, educational talks, and the opportunity to see animals from around the world, including New Zealand's native species.

2. Kelly Tarlton's Sea Life Aquarium

Website: https://www.kellytarltons.co.nz/ Description: Kelly Tarlton's Sea Life Aquarium offers families the chance to explore the marine world up close. Visitors can walk through an underwater tunnel, observe penguins in an Antarctic habitat, and even touch and feed some sea creatures in interactive exhibits.

3. MOTAT (Museum of Transport and Technology)

Website: https://www.motat.nz/ Description: MOTAT is an interactive museum featuring exhibits on transportation, technology, and innovation.

Families can explore vintage vehicles, trams, airplanes, and interactive science exhibits, making it a fun and educational destination for all ages.

4. Rainbow's End Theme Park

Website: https://rainbowsend.co.nz/ Description: Rainbow's End is New Zealand's largest theme park, offering over 20 thrilling rides and attractions suitable for all ages. From roller coasters and water rides to gentle rides for younger children, there's something for everyone at this exciting destination.

5. Tiritiri Matangi Island

Website: https://tiritirimatangi.org.nz/ Description: Tiritiri Matangi Island is a wildlife sanctuary and a great family-friendly destination for nature lovers. The island is home to many native bird species and offers beautiful walking trails, guided tours, and a lighthouse to explore.

6. Stardome Observatory and Planetarium

Website: https://www.stardome.org.nz/ Description: The Stardome Observatory and Planetarium offers families the opportunity to explore the universe through interactive exhibits, planetarium shows, and telescope viewings. It's an excellent way to spark children's interest in astronomy and science.

7. Butterfly Creek

Website: https://www.butterflycreek.co.nz/ Description: Butterfly Creek is a unique attraction featuring a tropical butterfly house, live crocodile exhibits, a dinosaur kingdom, and a variety of other animal exhibits. The park also offers a playground, miniature train rides, and a café, making it a great day out for families.

8. Whoa! Studios

Website: https://whoastudios.co.nz/ Description: Whoa! Studios is a family entertainment destination offering live theater performances, interactive workshops, and a unique urban playground. The park features a state-of-the-art studio where children can engage in creative activities such as puppetry, filmmaking, and storytelling.

9.   Cornwall Park
Website: https://cornwallpark.co.nz/ Description: Cornwall Park is a beautiful and spacious park in the heart of Auckland, featuring walking trails, picnic areas, playgrounds, and even farm animals. It's an ideal spot for families to relax, play, and enjoy outdoor activities.

10. Auckland Maritime Museum
Website: https://www.maritimemuseum.co.nz/ Description: The Auckland Maritime Museum showcases New Zealand's maritime history through interactive exhibits and displays. Families can explore historic vessels, learn about the nation's sailing history, and participate in hands-on activities and workshops.

Adventure and adrenaline-pumping experiences in Auckland

1.   SkyJump and SkyWalk
Website: https://www.sky.co.nz/skyjump-skywalk
Description: For thrill-seekers, the SkyJump and SkyWalk at the Sky Tower offer an adrenaline rush like no other. The SkyJump is a controlled base jump from 192 meters above the city, while the SkyWalk involves walking around the tower's narrow platform at the same height.

2.   Auckland Bridge Climb and Bungy
Website: https://www.bungy.co.nz/auckland-bridge
Description: The Auckland Bridge Climb provides a unique perspective on the city as you climb the iconic harbor bridge. For an added adrenaline kick take on the Auckland Bridge Bungy, a 40-meter jump with the option to touch the waters of the Waitematā Harbour.

3. Canyoning in the Waitakere Ranges

Website: https://www.awoladventures.co.nz/

Description: Canyoning in the Waitakere Ranges offers a thrilling adventure amidst stunning natural scenery. This guided experience includes abseiling down waterfalls, jumping into pools, and navigating through narrow canyons in a lush rainforest setting.

4. Jet Boating on the Waitematā Harbour

Website: https://www.aucklandjetboattours.co.nz/

Description: Experience high-speed thrills with a jet boat ride on the Waitematā Harbour. Hold on tight as the boat reaches speeds of up to 85 km/h, while performing sharp turns, spins, and power slides on the water.

5. Indoor Skydiving at iFLY

Website: https://www.iflynz.co.nz/

Description: iFLY offers the excitement of skydiving without jumping out of a plane. The indoor wind tunnel simulates the sensation of freefalling, providing a thrilling experience for both beginners and experienced skydivers.

6. Tree Adventures

Website: https://www.treeadventures.co.nz/

Description: Unleash your inner Tarzan at Tree Adventures, an outdoor high ropes course set in the picturesque Woodhill Forest. With various difficulty levels, you can traverse rope bridges, swing through the trees, and zip-line through the canopy.

7. Surfing at Piha Beach

Website: https://www.pihasurfacademy.com/

Description: Piha Beach, located on Auckland's rugged west coast, is a popular destination for surfing enthusiasts. Take a surf lesson or rent a board and ride the waves at this stunning black sand beach, known for its powerful surf and dramatic scenery.

8. Mountain Biking at Woodhill Forest

Website: https://www.bikeparks.co.nz/

Description: Woodhill Forest offers over 100 km of purpose-built mountain bike trails suitable for all skill levels. Rent a bike and helmet or bring your own, and explore the exhilarating terrain amidst a beautiful forest setting.

9. Paragliding and Hang Gliding

Website: https://www.adventureflights.co.nz/

Description: Take to the skies with a tandem paragliding or hang gliding experience, soaring above the stunning landscapes surrounding Auckland. With the guidance of an experienced pilot, you'll enjoy unparalleled views and a thrilling flight.

10. Sailing on an America's Cup Yacht

Website: https://www.exploregroup.co.nz/experiences/explore-sailing-auckland

Description: Experience the thrill of sailing on an authentic America's Cup yacht in the City of Sails. Join the crew and learn to navigate, trim the sails, or even take the helm as you cruise through the beautiful Waitematā Harbour.

Wellness and relaxation options in Auckland: spas, yoga, and meditation centers

1. East Day Spa

Website: https://www.eastdayspa.com/

Description: East Day Spa is a luxurious spa located in the heart of Auckland, offering a range of rejuvenating treatments, including massages, facials, body wraps, and more. The spa focuses on blending traditional Eastern healing techniques with modern Western therapies to create a unique wellness experience.

2. Chuan Spa at Cordis Auckland

Website: https://www.cordishotels.com/en/auckland/wellness/chuan-spa/

Description: Chuan Spa, located within the Cordis Auckland hotel, offers a holistic approach to wellness based on traditional Chinese medicine principles. Enjoy treatments such as massages, facials, and body scrubs, as well as access to spa facilities like saunas, steam rooms, and a heated rooftop pool.

3. The Spa at the Pullman Hotel

Website: https://www.pullmanauckland.co.nz/wellness/

Description: The Spa at the Pullman Hotel offers a tranquil sanctuary for relaxation and rejuvenation. Choose from a range of treatments, including massages, facials, and hydrotherapy, and enjoy the spa's facilities, including a heated indoor pool, sauna, and fitness center.

4. Bliss Reflexology

Website: https://www.blissreflexology.com/

Description: Bliss Reflexology specializes in traditional Chinese reflexology and therapeutic massage, aiming to restore balance and energy flow in the body. Their treatments focus on pressure points in the feet, hands, and ears to promote relaxation and healing.

5. Studio Red Yoga

Website: https://www.studioredyoga.com/

Description: Studio Red Yoga is a boutique yoga studio located in the city center, offering a variety of yoga styles, including Vinyasa, Yin, and Hot Yoga. The studio features a calming environment with state-of-the-art infrared heating and experienced instructors.

6. Auckland Meditation

Website: https://www.aucklandmeditation.com/

Description: Auckland Meditation offers meditation classes and workshops to help individuals develop mindfulness and reduce stress. They provide a range of techniques, such as guided visualization, mantra meditation, and breathwork, to suit different needs and preferences.

7. Golden Yogi

Website: https://goldenyogi.co.nz/

Description: Golden Yogi is a wellness studio in Takapuna, offering yoga, meditation, and holistic treatments. Their diverse class schedule includes Kundalini Yoga, Restorative Yoga, and Mindfulness Meditation, as well as workshops and special events.

8. Sanctuary Yoga and Wellness

Website: https://www.sanctuaryyogawellness.com/

Description: Sanctuary Yoga and Wellness is a boutique yoga studio in the suburb of Devonport, offering a range of classes, including Hatha, Vinyasa, and Yin Yoga. The studio also provides workshops, retreats, and wellness events to help deepen your practice and support a balanced lifestyle.

9. Urban Ashram

Website: https://www.urbanashram.co.nz/

Description: Urban Ashram is a tranquil yoga studio in Parnell, offering classes suitable for all levels and abilities. Choose from a variety of yoga styles, such as Vinyasa, Restorative, and Iyengar, and enjoy the serene atmosphere and experienced instructors.

10. The Floating Lotus

Website: https://www.thefloatinglotus.co.nz/

Description: The Floating Lotus offers flotation therapy, an effective relaxation and wellness technique. Floating in a sensory deprivation tank filled with Epsom salt-infused water can help reduce stress, ease muscle tension, and promote deep relaxation. The center also offers massage therapy and infrared sauna sessions.

LGBTQ+ friendly venues and events in Auckland

1. Family Bar & Club
Website: https://www.familybar.co.nz/
Description: Family Bar & Club is one of Auckland's most popular LGBTQ+ venues, offering a lively atmosphere, themed nights, and entertaining drag shows. Spread over two levels, the venue caters to various music tastes and moods, making it a great spot for a night out.

2. Caluzzi Bar and Cabaret
Website: https://www.caluzzi.co.nz/
Description: Caluzzi Bar and Cabaret offers an unforgettable dining and entertainment experience, featuring fabulous drag queens, cabaret performances, and interactive games. The venue is perfect for a fun night out, special occasions, or group events.

3. Garnet Station Tiny Theatre
Website: https://www.garnetstation.com/
Description: Garnet Station Tiny Theatre is a cozy and eclectic venue that hosts a variety of events, including LGBTQ+ themed plays, comedy, and storytelling. The venue also features a cafe and garden bar, making it a perfect spot to relax and enjoy the creative atmosphere.

4. The Eagle Bar
Website: https://www.eaglebar.nz/
Description: The Eagle Bar is a popular LGBTQ+ bar in Auckland's city center, offering a laid-back atmosphere, friendly staff, and regular events like karaoke nights and quiz nights. It's a great place to unwind with friends or meet new people.

5. K'Road (Karangahape Road)
Website: https://www.kroad.com/

Description: K'Road is a vibrant and diverse area known for its eclectic mix of bars, clubs, restaurants, and boutiques. The street has a rich history as a hub for Auckland's LGBTQ+ community and continues to be a popular destination for nightlife and events.

6. Auckland Pride Festival
Website: https://aucklandpride.org.nz/
Description: Auckland Pride Festival is an annual celebration of the LGBTQ+ community, featuring a wide range of events, including art exhibitions, theater performances, workshops, and the iconic Pride Parade. The festival aims to foster inclusion, diversity, and visibility for the LGBTQ+ community.

7. Ending HIV Big Gay Out
Website: https://www.biggayout.co.nz/
Description: Ending HIV Big Gay Out is New Zealand's largest LGBTQ+ event held annually at Coyle Park in Point Chevalier. The event features live music, drag performances, food stalls, and community organizations, providing a fun and inclusive atmosphere for all.

8. OUTLine NZ
Website: https://www.outline.org.nz/
Description: OUTLine NZ is a national LGBTQ+ organization offering support, information, and resources. They host regular events, workshops, and support groups, providing a safe space for the LGBTQ+ community to connect and access essential services.

9. Gay Ski Week NZ
Website: https://gayskiweeknz.com/
Description: Gay Ski Week NZ, held annually in Queenstown, is a week-long celebration of winter sports, parties, and entertainment. While not located in Auckland, this event attracts many visitors from the city and is a popular event within New Zealand's LGBTQ+ community.

10. Everybody Eats - LGBTQ+ Community Nights

Website: https://www.everybodyeats.nz/

Description: Everybody Eats is a pay-as-you-feel dining concept aimed at reducing food waste and building community connections. They host regular LGBTQ+ community nights, providing an inclusive space for people to share a meal and engage in conversation.

Museums and art galleries in Auckland

Auckland is home to a vibrant arts and culture scene, with a range of museums and art galleries showcasing the city's rich history and diverse creative talent. Whether you're interested in art, history, or science, there are plenty of museums and galleries to explore in Auckland. Here are some of the top museums and art galleries in the city:

- **Auckland War Memorial Museum**: The Auckland War Memorial Museum is one of the city's top cultural attractions, showcasing New Zealand's military history, natural history, and Maori culture. The museum's collections include more than 1.5 million objects and artifacts, including Maori carvings, textiles, and weapons, as well as displays on New Zealand's involvement in World War I and II. The museum also features a planetarium and natural history exhibits. Admission to the museum is NZD $25 for adults, with discounts available for children and families.

- **Auckland Art Gallery:** The Auckland Art Gallery is home to New Zealand's largest collection of art, including works by some of the country's most famous artists. The gallery's collections include European and American art, as well as contemporary and traditional Maori art. The gallery also hosts regular exhibitions and events, showcasing the work of both local and international artists. Admission to the gallery is free, with special exhibitions requiring a fee.

- **New Zealand Maritime Museum:** The New Zealand Maritime Museum is located in the Viaduct Harbour area and offers an insight into the country's maritime history and culture. The museum's exhibits include interactive displays, historic boats, and a range of artifacts related to New Zealand's seafaring past. Visitors can also take a guided tour of the harbor on a historic vessel. Admission to the museum is NZD $20 for adults, with discounts available for children and families.

- **MOTAT:** The Museum of Transport and Technology (MOTAT) is located in Auckland's Western Springs area and showcases the country's transport and technology history. The museum's exhibits include vintage cars, trains, and planes, as well as interactive displays on technology and science. Visitors can also take a tram ride through the museum's historic village. Admission to MOTAT is NZD $19 for adults, with discounts available for children and families.
- **Gus Fisher Gallery**: The Gus Fisher Gallery is a contemporary art gallery located in the central business district. The gallery showcases a range of works by both local and international artists, with a focus on contemporary art and design. Admission to the gallery is free.

Overall, Auckland offers a range of museums and art galleries to explore, showcasing the city's rich cultural history and diverse creative talent. By visiting these top museums and galleries in Auckland, you'll gain a deeper understanding of the city's history and culture, while also experiencing some of its most exciting artistic and cultural offerings.

Outdoor activities in Auckland (e.g., beaches, parks, hiking)

Auckland is renowned for its stunning natural beauty and offers a wide range of outdoor activities for visitors to enjoy. From hiking and biking to water sports and wildlife encounters, there's something for everyone in this amazing city. Here are some of the top outdoor activities to experience in Auckland, along with practical tips and information to help you make the most of your visit:

- **Hiking and Walking:** Auckland is home to a wide range of hiking trails and walking tracks, with something to suit all fitness levels and interests. Some of the top hiking trails include the Waitakere Ranges, the Rangitoto Summit Track, and the Mount Eden Summit Track. These trails offer stunning views of the city skyline, lush rainforest, and volcanic landscapes. When hiking, be sure to wear comfortable shoes and bring plenty of water and sunscreen.
- **Beaches:** Auckland is surrounded by beautiful beaches, making it a popular destination for water sports and beach activities. Some of the top beaches in the area include Piha Beach, Takapuna Beach, and Orewa Beach. Visitors can enjoy swimming, surfing, kayaking, and paddleboarding, as well as relaxing on the sand and soaking up the sun. When visiting the beaches, be sure to check the weather and surf conditions before heading out, and always swim between the flags.
- **Water Sports:** In addition to beach activities, Auckland offers a wide range of water sports, including sailing, fishing, and sea kayaking. Visitors can rent a boat or join a guided tour to explore the Hauraki Gulf and its many islands. The Gulf is home to a diverse range of marine life, including dolphins, whales, and seabirds. When participating in water sports, be sure to wear a life jacket and follow all safety guidelines.
- **Wildlife Encounters:** Auckland is home to a wealth of unique wildlife, including kiwis, dolphins, and penguins. Visitors can take guided tours to see these animals in their natural habitats, or visit one of the city's many wildlife sanctuaries, such as the Auckland Zoo or the Tiritiri Matangi Island Wildlife Sanctuary. When visiting wildlife areas, be sure to follow all guidelines and respect the animals' natural habitats.
- **Cycling:** Auckland is a bike-friendly city, with a wide range of cycling trails and bike rental options available. Visitors can rent a bike and explore the city's many parks and waterfront areas, or join a guided bike tour to see the city's top attractions. When cycling, be sure to wear a helmet and follow all traffic laws and safety guidelines.

Overall, Auckland offers a wide range of outdoor activities for visitors to enjoy, from hiking and biking to water sports and wildlife encounters. By taking advantage of these amazing opportunities, you'll be able to experience the city's stunning natural beauty and diverse cultural offerings, while also getting some exercise and fresh air. Be sure to plan ahead and pack appropriately for your chosen activity, and always follow safety guidelines to ensure a safe and enjoyable experience.

Shopping and dining in Auckland

Shopping and dining are two of the top attractions in Auckland, offering visitors a wide range of options to suit all tastes and budgets. From high-end fashion boutiques and designer stores to local markets and street food stalls, Auckland has it all. Here's a closer look at what to expect when shopping and dining in Auckland:

Shopping in Auckland:
- **Queen Street:** Queen Street is Auckland's main shopping district, featuring a range of high-end fashion boutiques, department stores, and souvenir shops. Visitors can find everything from designer clothing and accessories to locally made crafts and gifts.
- **Britomart:** Britomart is a stylish precinct located in the heart of Auckland's CBD, offering a range of high-end fashion and lifestyle stores, as well as trendy cafes and restaurants. Visitors can shop for designer clothing and accessories, as well as unique homewares and gifts.
- **Auckland Night Markets:** Auckland is home to a range of night markets, offering a variety of street food, live entertainment, and local crafts. Some of the top markets include the Takapuna Night Markets, the Auckland Fish Market, and the Parnell Farmers' Market.

Dining in Auckland:
- **Ponsonby Road:** Ponsonby Road is one of Auckland's top dining destinations, offering a range of restaurants and cafes serving up

delicious cuisine from around the world. Visitors can choose from Italian, Japanese, Thai, and more, as well as local New Zealand fare.

- **Viaduct Harbour:** Viaduct Harbour is another popular dining destination, offering stunning waterfront views and a range of restaurants and bars. Visitors can enjoy fresh seafood, international cuisine, and trendy cocktail bars, all while taking in the harbor views.
- **Food Trucks:** Auckland is home to a range of food trucks, offering a variety of street food options from around the world. Some of the top food truck locations include the Auckland Night Markets and the Wynyard Quarter.

Overall, shopping and dining are two of the top attractions in Auckland, offering visitors a wide range of options to explore. Whether you're looking for high-end fashion boutiques or local street food, Auckland has something to suit every taste and budget. Be sure to explore the city's many shopping and dining districts, as well as its unique markets and food trucks, for a truly authentic Auckland experience.

Shopping in Auckland

Prices in New Zealand are high and you will find that you will be better off buying goods before you arrive. According to the Numbeo cost of living survey, New Zealand is the 14th most expensive country in the world. Cosmetics, clothing and other consumer goods will cost far more here than they will in Europe or North America - though they are slightly cheaper than in Australia if you're visiting both countries as part of a bigger trip. Souvenir shops are plentiful with the most popular items being wool clothing, Maori style jewelry and manuka honey. The most popular Maori item is the pendant - called a pounamu - and the most traditional ones are made of jade. Different shapes have different meanings, and culturally it is only good luck if someone else gives one to you as a gift.
In terms of shopping districts, you have a few options:

- Queen Street and Britomart

Queen Street has your general high street style shops - Topshop, Cotton O
and Factories are all based here and popular with locals. There are also son
interesting malls in Victorian Era buildings hidden on the street. Typically
they will have a single entrance door and you can enter into a larger space
with multiple shops. These are typically run by and for the Asian communit
so expect delicious Chinese food and markets selling clothes from various
places in Asia. There are also a bunch of souvenir shops here, however, the
can be more expensive due to the central location.

Britomart is a district that begins at the end of Queen Street close to the
waterfront. This is a much more upmarket area and features a number of
designer brands - both NZ and international - as well as high concept café
and restaurants. Many of the stores here open until 9 pm so it is a great
option for shopping later in the day, and the restaurants frequently garner
awards and great reviews.

- Ponsonby Road

Just outside of the CBD, Ponsonby Road has a range of boutique style sho
selling clothes, furniture, and food. The souvenirs here are a lot more uniqu
than the average tourist shops and you can find a gift more tailored to you
friends and family at home. Shops have a range of prices but are generally
little bit more expensive than the high street brands on Queen Street.
Nevertheless, the quality is very good and there are plenty of cool
restaurants and food courts to relax in after a few hours of shopping.

- Karangahape Road (K Road)

K Road, once a no-go area of the city, has now become Auckland's
alternative area attracting hipster types, the LGBT community, and creative
Here you will find op shops - the Kiwi way of saying thrift store - that is
meticulously curated and will give you a wide range of clothes, gifts and Br
a brac that act as a museum of New Zealand cultural history in themselves.
For a more retro souvenir or outfit, this is the best location in the city to

have a look. Unlike other shops in New Zealand, op shops are very reasonably priced and comparable with thrift stores in Europe and the United States.

- Newmarket

Newmarket has a good combination of mid-range and high-end concept stores and showcases the best in New Zealand design. If you want to take a look at the hottest young New Zealand fashion designers, this is the area to come to. There are also some high street stores - most notably Lush and K'Mart - but this area is more often frequented by locals looking to support New Zealand brands by purchasing high-quality fashion and furniture. There's also a great café district, and some of the best coffee in the city can be found here. Neighbouring Grafton has a slightly different vibe, with more student-oriented shops and Asian supermarkets. Nevertheless, it is an interesting suburb to visit to experience a different side of the city from Newmarket.

- Takapuna

Though Takapuna does not offer anything unique - it has the same kind of vibe as Ponsonby, with some streets that offer more high street brands - it is a great option if you are living in the North Shore. You could easily spend an entire day in the area. Not only are there great shops and award-winning restaurants, one of the most popular beaches in the city is based in Takapuna and offers an unbeatable view of Rangitoto - the volcanic island that looms over the city. For a more relaxed, stretched-out shopping experience, we recommend Takapuna as a good combination of all the other Auckland shopping areas.

Nightlife in Auckland

Auckland is a vibrant and exciting city with a lively nightlife scene, offering visitors a range of options for entertainment and socializing. From trendy bars and nightclubs to live music venues and comedy shows, there's something for everyone in this amazing city. Here's a closer look at what to expect when experiencing the nightlife in Auckland:

Bars and Nightclubs:
1. **Karangahape Road:** Karangahape Road, also known as K Road, is one of Auckland's top destinations for nightlife, featuring a range of bars and nightclubs catering to all tastes and preferences. Visitors can enjoy everything from indie rock bands to electronic DJs, as well as craft beer and artisan cocktails.
2. **Ponsonby Road:** Ponsonby Road is another popular destination for nightlife, offering a range of bars and clubs featuring live music and DJs. Visitors can enjoy a range of music genres, from reggae to hip hop, as well as local craft beer and wine.
3. **Viaduct Harbour:** Viaduct Harbour is a stylish waterfront area with a range of bars and nightclubs offering stunning harbor views and a sophisticated atmosphere. Visitors can enjoy craft cocktails, international wines, and top-notch DJs, all while taking in the beautiful surroundings.

Live Music Venues:
1. **The Civic:** The Civic is one of Auckland's most iconic live music venues, offering a range of concerts and performances throughout the year. Visitors can enjoy everything from classical music to rock bands, as well as Broadway musicals and dance performances.
2. **The Powerstation:** The Powerstation is another popular live music venue, featuring a range of local and international acts across a variety of music genres. Visitors can enjoy everything from indie rock to electronic dance music, as well as comedy shows and special events.

Comedy Shows:

1. **The Classic Comedy Club:** The Classic Comedy Club is Auckland's top destination for comedy shows, featuring a range of local and international comedians performing stand-up, improv, and sketch comedy. Visitors can enjoy drinks and snacks while laughing along to some of the city's funniest performers.

Overall, Auckland offers a range of options for nightlife entertainment, from trendy bars and nightclubs to live music venues and comedy shows. Whether you're looking to dance the night away or enjoy a more laid-back atmosphere, Auckland has something to suit every taste and preference. Be sure to explore the city's many nightlife districts and venues for an unforgettable experience.

Useful Information on the Places

Place	Website	Address	Cost
Sky Tower	https://www.skycityauckland.co.nz/en/sky-tower/	Corner Victoria and Federal Streets, Auckland 1010	Adults: NZD $32, Children (6-14 years): NZD $13
Auckland Harbour Bridge Climb	https://www.ajhackett.com/auckland/	105 Curran Street, Westhaven, Auckland 1010	Adults: NZD $195
Waiheke Island	https://www.waiheke.co.nz/	Waiheke Island, Auckland	Ferry: NZD $42-50
Auckland Zoo	https://www.aucklandzoo.co.nz/	99 Motions Road, Western Springs, Auckland 1022	Adults: NZD $28, Children (4-14 years): NZD $12

Place	Website	Address	Cost
Rangitoto Island	https://www.doc.govt.nz/parks-and-recreation/places-to-go/auckland/places/rangitoto-island/	Rangitoto Island, Auckland	Ferry: NZD $36-40
Kelly Tarlton's Sea Life Aquarium	https://www.visitsealife.com/auckland/	23 Tamaki Drive, Orakei, Auckland 1071	Adults: NZD $39, Children (3-15 years): NZD $22
Auckland Museum	https://www.aucklandmuseum.com/	The Auckland Domain, Parnell, Auckland 1010	Adults: NZD $25
Auckland Art Gallery	https://www.aucklandartgallery.com/	Corner Kitchener and Wellesley Streets, Auckland 1010	Free (special exhibitions may have a fee)
New Zealand Maritime Museum	https://www.maritimemuseum.co.nz/	Corner Quay and Hobson Streets, Auckland 1010	Adults: NZD $20
Museum of Transport and Technology	https://www.motat.org.nz/	805 Great North Road, Western Springs, Auckland 1022	Adults: NZD $19
Gus Fisher Gallery	https://www.gusfishergallery.auckland.ac.nz/	74 Shortland Street, Auckland 1010	Free

Note: Prices listed are as of the time of writing and are subject to change. Please check the respective websites for up-to-date information on pricing and admission.

5.Day trips from Auckland

While Auckland is a fantastic destination in itself, there are also many incredible day trip options available for those looking to explore more of New Zealand's North Island. From the rugged beauty of the Coromandel Peninsula to the charming towns of the Bay of Islands, there's no shortage of amazing sights and experiences just a short drive or ferry ride from Auckland. In this section, we'll highlight some of the top day trip options from Auckland, along with practical tips and information to help you plan your adventure.

Waiheke Island

One of the most popular day trip destinations from Auckland is Waiheke Island, a beautiful island located just a short ferry ride from downtown Auckland. Known for its stunning beaches, world-class vineyards, and laid-back vibe, Waiheke Island offers visitors a chance to escape the hustle and bustle of the city and experience the natural beauty of New Zealand's North Island.

Once on the island, visitors can explore a range of activities and attractions, including:
- Vineyard Tours: Waiheke Island is home to over 30 wineries, making it a popular destination for wine lovers. Visitors can take guided tours of the island's vineyards, sample some of the region's finest wines, and enjoy stunning views of the island's lush landscape.
- Beaches: Waiheke Island is home to a number of beautiful beaches, including Oneroa Beach, Onetangi Beach, and Palm Beach. Visitors can swim, sunbathe, and enjoy a range of water sports, such as kayaking and paddleboarding.
- Hiking: Waiheke Island offers a range of hiking trails, allowing visitors to explore the island's rugged coastline and lush forests. Some of the top

trails include the Headland Sculpture Walk and the Waiheke Island Eco Trail.

- Art Galleries: Waiheke Island is known for its vibrant arts scene, with a range of galleries and studios showcasing the work of local artists. Visitors can explore the island's galleries, attend art events and festivals and purchase unique pieces to take home as souvenirs.

There are several ferry operators that offer service to Waiheke Island from Auckland, with departures available from downtown Auckland and Devonport. Ferry tickets typically cost between NZD $42-50 for a round-trip ticket, with a journey time of approximately 35-45 minutes each way. Overall, a day trip to Waiheke Island offers visitors a chance to experience the natural beauty and unique culture of New Zealand's North Island. Whether you're a wine lover, beachgoer, hiker, or art enthusiast, Waiheke Island has something to offer for everyone. Be sure to plan ahead and make the most of your time on the island, whether it's exploring the vineyards, soaking up the sun on the beach, or discovering the island's vibrant arts scene.

Rangitoto Island

Another popular day trip destination from Auckland is Rangitoto Island, a volcanic island located just off the coast of Auckland. Known for its rugged terrain, unique lava caves, and stunning views of the Hauraki Gulf, Rangitoto Island offers visitors a chance to explore the natural wonders of New Zealand's North Island.

Once on the island, visitors can explore a range of activities and attractions including:

- Hiking: Rangitoto Island offers a range of hiking trails, allowing visitors to explore the island's volcanic landscape and unique flora and fauna.

The summit hike is a popular option, offering stunning views of the Hauraki Gulf and surrounding islands.

- Lava Caves: Rangitoto Island is home to a number of unique lava caves, formed by the island's volcanic activity. Visitors can explore these caves with guided tours, learning about the island's geology and history.
- Beaches: Rangitoto Island offers a range of beautiful beaches, including Islington Bay and Mackenzie Bay. Visitors can swim, sunbathe, and enjoy a range of water sports, such as kayaking and paddleboarding.
- Wildlife: Rangitoto Island is home to a range of unique wildlife, including native birds, lizards, and insects. Visitors can explore the island's flora and fauna with guided tours or on their own.

To get to Rangitoto Island, visitors can take a ferry from downtown Auckland, with several ferry operators offering regular service. The ferry ride takes approximately 25-30 minutes each way, with round-trip tickets typically costing between NZD $36-40.

Overall, a day trip to Rangitoto Island offers visitors a chance to experience the natural beauty and unique geology of New Zealand's North Island. Whether you're a hiker, beachgoer, or wildlife enthusiast, Rangitoto Island has something to offer for everyone. Be sure to plan ahead and make the most of your time on the island, whether it's exploring the lava caves, hiking to the summit, or soaking up the sun on the beach.

Waitomo Caves

Waitomo Caves is a popular day trip destination from Auckland, located approximately two and a half hours south of the city. Known for its stunning underground caves and unique glowworms, Waitomo Caves offers visitors a chance to explore the natural wonders of New Zealand's North Island. Once at the caves, visitors can explore a range of activities and attractions, including:

- **Cave Tours**: Waitomo Caves offers a range of cave tours, allowing visitors to explore the underground caverns and learn about the geology and history of the region. The most popular tour is the Glowworm Cave Tour, which includes a boat ride through the Glowworm Grotto, where visitors can see thousands of glowworms lighting up the cave.
- **Adventure Tours:** Waitomo Caves also offers a range of adventure tours, such as abseiling, black water rafting, and zip lining. These tours offer visitors a chance to explore the caves in a more active and adventurous way.
- **Natural Wonders:** In addition to the caves themselves, Waitomo Caves is also home to a range of other natural wonders, such as the limestone formations and underground rivers. Visitors can explore these natural wonders with guided tours or on their own.

To get to Waitomo Caves from Auckland, you can drive or take a bus, with several bus companies offering regular service to the region. Day tours are also available, which include transport from Auckland and guided tours of the caves.

Overall, a day trip to Waitomo Caves offers visitors a chance to experience the unique geology and natural wonders of New Zealand's North Island. Whether you're interested in cave tours, adventure activities, or simply soaking up the stunning scenery, Waitomo Caves has something to offer for everyone. Be sure to plan ahead and make the most of your time in the region, whether it's exploring the underground caves, going on an adventure tour, or simply enjoying the natural beauty of the area.

Bay of Islands

The Bay of Islands is a popular day trip destination from Auckland, located approximately three hours north of the city. Known for its stunning coastline, beautiful beaches, and rich history, the Bay of Islands offers visitors a chance to explore the natural and cultural wonders of New Zealand's North Island.

Once in the Bay of Islands, visitors can explore a range of activities and attractions, including:

- **Historic Sites:** The Bay of Islands is rich in history, with a number of historic sites and landmarks to explore. These include the Waitangi Treaty Grounds, where the Treaty of Waitangi was signed between the British Crown and Maori chiefs, as well as the Russell Museum, which tells the story of the town's colorful past.
- **Beaches and Water Sports:** The Bay of Islands is home to a range of beautiful beaches, offering visitors a chance to swim, sunbathe, and enjoy a range of water sports, such as kayaking, snorkeling, and sailing.
- **Wildlife:** The Bay of Islands is home to a range of unique wildlife, including dolphins, whales, and seabirds. Visitors can take boat tours to see these animals up close, as well as explore the region's many nature reserves and parks.

To get to the Bay of Islands from Auckland, visitors can drive or take a bus, with several bus companies offering regular service to the region. Day tours are also available, which include transport from Auckland and guided tours of the region.

Overall, a day trip to the Bay of Islands offers visitors a chance to experience the natural beauty and rich history of New Zealand's North Island. Whether you're interested in exploring historic sites, relaxing on the beach, or seeing unique wildlife up close, the Bay of Islands has something to offer for everyone. Be sure to plan ahead and make the most of your time in the region, whether it's visiting historic sites, going on a boat tour, or simply enjoying the stunning scenery.

Coromandel Peninsula

The Coromandel Peninsula is a stunning day trip destination from Auckland, located approximately two and a half hours east of the city. Known for its rugged coastline, beautiful beaches, and lush forests, the Coromandel Peninsula offers visitors a chance to explore the natural wonders of New Zealand's North Island.

Once on the peninsula, visitors can explore a range of activities and attractions, including:

- Beaches: The Coromandel Peninsula is home to some of New Zealand's most beautiful beaches, such as Hot Water Beach and Cathedral Cove. Visitors can swim, sunbathe, and enjoy a range of water sports, such as surfing and kayaking.
- Hiking: The Coromandel Peninsula offers a range of hiking trails, allowing visitors to explore the region's lush forests and rugged coastline. The Coromandel Coastal Walkway is a popular option, offering stunning views of the ocean and surrounding landscape.
- Hot Springs: The Coromandel Peninsula is home to a number of natural hot springs, such as the Hot Water Beach. Visitors can dig their own hot pools in the sand and relax in the warm water.
- Arts and Crafts: The Coromandel Peninsula is known for its vibrant arts and crafts scene, with a range of galleries and studios showcasing the work of local artists. Visitors can explore the region's galleries, attend art events and festivals, and purchase unique pieces to take home as souvenirs.

To get to the Coromandel Peninsula from Auckland, visitors can drive or take a bus, with several bus companies offering regular service to the region. Day tours are also available, which include transport from Auckland and guided tours of the region.

Overall, a day trip to the Coromandel Peninsula offers visitors a chance to experience the natural beauty and unique culture of New Zealand's North

Island. Whether you're interested in beaches, hiking, hot springs, or arts and crafts, the Coromandel Peninsula has something to offer for everyone. Be sure to plan ahead and make the most of your time in the region, whether it's digging your own hot pool on Hot Water Beach, hiking the Coromandel Coastal Walkway, or exploring the region's vibrant arts scene.

Hobbiton Movie Set

Website: https://www.hobbitontours.com/
Description: The Hobbiton Movie Set, located near Matamata, is a must-visit destination for fans of The Lord of the Rings and The Hobbit film trilogies. Experience the magic of the Shire as you explore the 12-acre set, featuring 44 Hobbit holes, including Bilbo Baggins' home, Bag End.

The guided tour takes you through the movie set, with fascinating insights into the making of the films and the attention to detail that brought the Shire to life. Wander through the lush gardens, past the mill, and over the double-arched bridge before stopping for a drink at the Green Dragon Inn. The inn, a replica of the one featured in the movies, offers a selection of beverages, including Southfarthing ale and cider.

Getting there: Hobbiton is approximately a 2-hour drive from Auckland. There are also organized day tours available from Auckland, which include transportation, a guided tour of the set, and often a visit to the nearby Waitomo Caves. These tours typically last around 8-10 hours, depending on the itinerary.

Tips:
- Book your tickets in advance, as tours can sell out quickly, especially during peak tourist season.
- Wear comfortable walking shoes and bring a camera to capture the picturesque scenery.

- Check the weather forecast before your visit and dress accordingly, as most of the tour takes place outdoors.
- If you have extra time, consider exploring the charming town of Matamata and its surrounding countryside.

6.Cultural experiences in Auckland

New Zealand is a country with a rich and diverse cultural heritage, shaped by its indigenous Maori population, European settlers, and more recent waves of immigration from around the world. Auckland, as the largest city in New Zealand, offers visitors a range of opportunities to experience the country's unique cultural heritage, from traditional Maori performances to contemporary art exhibits. In this section, we'll highlight some of the top cultural experiences to be had in Auckland, along with practical tips and information to help you make the most of your time in the city. Whether you're interested in learning about Maori culture, exploring the city's museums and galleries, or attending a live performance, Auckland has something to offer for everyone.

Maori culture in Auckland

The Maori people are the indigenous population of New Zealand, and their culture and traditions have played a significant role in shaping the country's history and identity. In Auckland, visitors can experience Maori culture in a number of ways, from visiting traditional Maori villages to attending cultural performances and exhibits.

One of the top Maori cultural experiences in Auckland is a visit to the Auckland War Memorial Museum, which features a dedicated Maori section showcasing Maori artifacts, artwork, and cultural displays. Visitors can learn about Maori history and traditions, as well as the impact of European colonization on the Maori population.

Another popular Maori cultural experience in Auckland is attending a live performance, such as a haka or cultural dance show. Many venues throughout the city offer these performances, providing visitors with a chance to see Maori culture in action and learn more about its significance. Visiting a traditional Maori village is also a great way to experience Maori culture firsthand. There are several villages located within easy reach of Auckland, such as Tamaki Maori Village and Te Puia Maori Village. Visitors can learn about Maori customs and traditions, participate in traditional activities, and enjoy a traditional Maori feast.

Overall, experiencing Maori culture is an important part of any trip to New Zealand, and Auckland offers visitors a range of opportunities to do so. Whether you're interested in history, art, or performance, there's no shortage of ways to learn about and experience the unique and vibrant culture of the Maori people in Auckland.

Festivals and events in Auckland

Auckland is a city with a vibrant and diverse cultural scene, and there are a range of festivals and events held throughout the year to celebrate this diversity. From music and art to food and wine, there's always something going on in Auckland to keep visitors entertained.

One of the most popular events on the Auckland calendar is the Auckland Arts Festival, held every two years in March. The festival showcases a range of local and international music, theater, dance, and visual arts performances, as well as street performances and free events for the public.

Another popular event in Auckland is the Auckland Lantern Festival, held annually in February to celebrate the Chinese New Year. The festival features a range of colorful lantern displays, traditional food and drink, and cultural performances.

Food and wine lovers will enjoy the Taste of Auckland festival, held in November, which features some of the city's best chefs and restaurants showcasing their cuisine, as well as wine and beer tastings and other culinary events.

Music lovers won't want to miss the annual Auckland City Limits music festival, which features a lineup of local and international musicians across a range of genres.

Other notable festivals and events in Auckland include the Pasifika Festival, celebrating Pacific Island culture and heritage, and the Auckland Diwali Festival, celebrating the Hindu festival of lights.
Whether you're interested in music, art, food, or culture, there's always something to celebrate and enjoy in Auckland. Be sure to check the event calendar when planning your trip, and book tickets or make reservations early to ensure you don't miss out on the festivities.

Art and music scene in Auckland

Auckland has a vibrant and dynamic art and music scene, with a range of galleries, museums, and music venues to explore. Whether you're interested in contemporary art or classical music, there's something for everyone in Auckland's creative community.

One of the top art destinations in Auckland is the Auckland Art Gallery Toi o Tamaki, located in the heart of the city. The gallery houses a collection of over 15,000 works of art, with a focus on New Zealand and Pacific art, as well as contemporary and international art. The gallery also hosts a range of exhibitions and events throughout the year, showcasing the work of local and international artists.

Another popular art destination in Auckland is the street art scene, which can be found throughout the city's laneways and neighborhoods. The Karangahape Road area is particularly known for its colorful and vibrant street art, with new works popping up all the time.

For music lovers, Auckland offers a range of venues and events to enjoy. The Civic Theatre is a beautiful historic venue that hosts a range of performances, from musicals and plays to concerts and comedy shows. The Auckland Philharmonia Orchestra is another top music destination in the city, offering classical concerts throughout the year.

If you're interested in live music, Auckland has a range of venues to choose from, such as the iconic Powerstation, which has hosted some of the biggest names in music over the years. Other popular music venues include The Tuning Fork, Neck of the Woods, and Whammy Bar.

Overall, Auckland's art and music scene is a vibrant and exciting part of the city's cultural landscape. Whether you're interested in exploring the city's galleries and museums, or catching a live music performance, there's always something new and exciting to discover in Auckland's creative community.

Heritage walks and architectural landmarks

Heritage walks and architectural landmarks
1.   Auckland Heritage Walks
Website: https://www.heritageetours.co.nz/ Description: Auckland Heritage Walks offer guided walking tours that showcase the city's rich history and architectural landmarks. Led by knowledgeable guides, these tours explore areas such as the city center, Parnell, and Devonport, highlighting significant buildings, monuments, and historical sites.

2.   Britomart Precinct
Website: https://britomart.org/ Description: The Britomart Precinct is a vibrant area in downtown Auckland that combines historic architecture with modern design. Explore the beautifully restored heritage buildings, such as the former Chief Post Office and the Customs House, which now house boutique shops, restaurants, and offices.

3. Alberton House

Website: https://www.heritage.org.nz/places/places-to-visit/auckland-region/alberton Description: Alberton House is a beautifully preserved 19th-century mansion that offers a glimpse into the life of an affluent colonial family. The house features intricate architecture, lavish interiors, and picturesque gardens, making it a fascinating destination for history and architecture enthusiasts.

4. Highwic House

Website: https://www.heritage.org.nz/places/places-to-visit/auckland-region/highwic Description: Highwic House is another example of Auckland's architectural heritage, showcasing a Gothic Revival style. The house, once home to a wealthy 19th-century family, is now open to the public and features original furnishings, decorative art, and manicured gardens.

Performing arts: theater, dance, and concerts

1. Auckland Live

Website: https://www.aucklandlive.co.nz/ Description: Auckland Live is a major organization responsible for managing some of the city's most iconic performing arts venues, such as the Aotea Centre, The Civic, and the Bruce Mason Centre. Check their website for a schedule of upcoming theater, dance, and concert performances.

2. Q Theatre

Website: https://www.qtheatre.co.nz/ Description: Q Theatre is a contemporary performing arts hub in the city center, hosting a variety of local and international productions. The venue showcases theater, dance, and music performances, as well as comedy and other live events.

3. The Basement Theatre

Website: https://www.basementtheatre.co.nz/ Description: The Basement Theatre is an intimate venue dedicated to supporting emerging artists and innovative productions. With a focus on showcasing new works, the theater offers a diverse program of performances, including plays, dance, and comedy.

4. Auckland Philharmonia Orchestra

Website: https://www.apo.co.nz/ Description: The Auckland Philharmonia Orchestra (APO) is the city's leading professional orchestra, performing a wide range of classical, contemporary, and film music. The APO regularly collaborates with local and international artists, presenting concerts at various venues across Auckland.

5. Auckland Theatre Company

Website: https://www.atc.co.nz/ Description: Auckland Theatre Company is one of New Zealand's leading professional theater companies, producing a diverse range of contemporary and classic plays. Their productions often take place at the ASB Waterfront Theatre, a state-of-the-art venue located i the Wynyard Quarter.

7.Tours and activities that can be pre-booked

(https://pixabay.com/en/maori-painted-warrior-new-zealand-2151594/)

- **Auckland Maori Luxury Tour**

This is a great way to get a more private experience in modern Maori culture and the history that led to the current situation. This tour is great as you still get a taste of Auckland and the important attractions, but the Maori perspective enriches your understanding of the city. You will be taken through the most important multicultural sites in the city, as well as to Auckland's west coast to see some unique beaches and treks, and of course, you will be given information about volcanoes and how they related to Maori culture. The tour includes lunch, snacks, and drinks making it a great value day trip.

- **Piha Beach Day Trip and Shuttle Service**

The Waitakere ranges feature lush vegetation, waterfalls and wild beaches. This day trip takes you from Auckland to Piha beach whilst touring around the stunning region to the west of the city. Piha Beach is very popular with both locals and tourists and the local area will give you an interesting insight into the real New Zealand culture that exists outside of the city. This is a very basic tour with pick up, drop off and a local guide packed with suggestions – however, it is a great option if you want to explore the region at your own pace without having to worry about how you are going to get there.

(https://pixabay.com/en/house-home-quirky-movie-hobbit-2616607/)

- **Hobbiton and Waitomo Caves Guided Coach Tour from Auckland**

Lord of the Rings fan? Since the movies, and subsequent Hobbit trilogy, were created across the country, Kiwis have made a booming industry out of taking tourists to the key filming locations. The most famous is Hobbiton, which was preserved after the film for the Hobbit movies finished. This tour will take you to the Hobbit holes, and you will also receive lunch at the Green Dragon Inn.

The tour will also guide you to Waitomo Caves, and important natural sight in New Zealand where you can see glow worms. The tour includes entry into Hobbiton and the caves, lunch and a morning snack, transport to all of the locations and WiFi onboard the bus so you can share your adventure with your friends back home.

- Bay of Islands Day Tour with Dolphin Watching Cruise

North of Auckland, the Bay of Islands area is a gorgeous collection of seaside towns with beautiful beaches and picturesque views. You will be able to enjoy the oft-ignored northern bush before discovering the beautiful beaches of the edge of New Zealand.

Whilst in Paihia, the main town in the Bay of Islands, you will also get to enjoy a scenic boat cruise to the northernmost point of New Zealand, as well as have the opportunity to spot some dolphins swimming off the coast. The tour includes pick up and drop off and admission onto the boat.

- Waiheke Island Wine Tasting Tour from Auckland

Located in Auckland's Hauraki Gulf, Waiheke Island is an interesting community combining hippies, wealthy pensioners and holidaying Aucklanders amongst the beautiful volcanic landscape and wide beaches. It is also an important wine region for New Zealand. This tour will take you to the island to sample some of the finest wines the region has to offer. The tour includes a return ferry from Britomart, an all-day bus pass around the island, some light snacks and three premium wine tastings at different vineyards across the island. Live like a kiwi socialite for a day and taste why New Zealand wine has become world famous.

8. Top tips for traveling to Auckland

- New Zealanders and Australians generally get on well with each other, and most insults about either side are generally meant in good jest. Nevertheless, Kiwis are fiercely independent and visitors should avoid making comparisons between the two countries - particularly if it is more in favor of Australia. Treat them as separate countries with different experiences to offer, even if the cultures may initially seem similar to many tourists.
- Politeness is highly valued across the country, and Aucklanders are just as likely to take it seriously as others in the country. Always say please and thank you, even if it may seem unnecessary. Other customs include removing your shoes when entering someone's home, immediately telling someone where the toilets are if they are visiting you and taking extreme care when moving on public transport.
- Māori cultural experiences can be a great way to further enrich your visit to Auckland and experience a culture entirely different from everyday Auckland life. Nevertheless, there are some customs which should be observed. Generally, you will be informed of these before you begin the experience, and you should always follow them. Do not laugh at any of the Māori dances and procedures or the Haka. These are core to Māori culture and the indigenous population has fought hard to be respected.
- The "Keep New Zealand Beautiful" campaign was a very successful attempt to make Kiwis more ecologically aware. Littering will not be tolerated, so always be sure to bin your garbage.
- Smoking is not very common amongst the local population, and many areas of the city have been designated smoke-free zones. As a rule of thumb, if you do not see anyone else smoking it is best that you also try not to. Ask your accommodation where the nearest area to safely smoke is if you are a smoker. Cigarette prices are also extremely high and are due to reach a minimum of NZ$30 by 2020.

- When arriving in New Zealand you will be given a rather lengthy customs declaration form. Due to unique wildlife, New Zealand has very strict biohazard laws and restricts what you can and cannot bring into the country. If you are in doubt about an item, declare it anyway and the customs officers will happily advise you on whether you can keep it or get rid of it. There is no fine for declaring items that are safe, but there is a hefty fine attached to not declaring any items that are prohibited.
- Auckland is generally a safe city but has somewhat more safety concerns than the rest of the country. As with most cities around the world, avoid public parks at night. The areas around Queen Street, Karangahape Road (K Road) and Ponsonby Road may get quite rowdy at night, and some caution should be taken when out and about after dark in these areas. Also, make sure to keep all your valuables locked up, and if you have a car make sure it is secure. There has been a slight increase in burglaries in the city due to the housing crisis, but these generally target residential areas.
- New Zealand prides itself on being a society without a class system. Whilst this is only partially true, it is considered garish to display or talk about your wealth. Frugality is valued and you are expected to stay humble, even if you are a millionaire. Avoid flashy jewelry and never talk about money. You will be much more respected for displaying the Kiwi 'No. 8 Wire Spirit' and talking about frugality and how to fix broken items.
- If you want to go out for a drink you will need to take your passport. Bars will only accept NZ Driver Licences and Identity Cards, so all overseas citizens need to take a passport. If you are staying in New Zealand for a longer period of time you can apply for a citizen's card, however, this is a long and expensive process.

Useful Apps to Download

AT Mobile
Website: https://at.govt.nz/bus-train-ferry/more-services/mobile-services/
Description: AT Mobile is the official public transportation app for Auckland
providing information on buses, trains, and ferries. The app offers real-time
schedules, route planning, fare information, and service updates, making it
an essential tool for navigating the city's public transportation system.

Uber or Ola
Website: https://www.uber.com/nz/en/ or https://www.olacabs.com/nz
Description: Uber and Ola are popular ridesharing services in Auckland,
offering a convenient alternative to traditional taxis. Both apps allow you to
book a ride, track your driver, and pay for your trip seamlessly through the
app.

Neat Places
Website: https://neatplaces.co.nz/
Description: Neat Places is a curated guide to the best spots in Auckland,
including restaurants, cafes, bars, shops, and attractions. The app features
local recommendations and insider tips, helping you discover hidden gems
and unique experiences throughout the city.

CamperMate
Website: https://www.campermate.co.nz/
Description: CamperMate is a useful app for travelers exploring New Zealand
by campervan or car. The app provides information on campgrounds, petrol
stations, public restrooms, and other essential facilities, making it a valuable
resource for road trips and day trips from Auckland.

WeatherWatch
Website: https://www.weatherwatch.co.nz/
Description: WeatherWatch is a New Zealand-specific weather app, offering
accurate and up-to-date forecasts for Auckland and the surrounding

regions. The app provides detailed weather information, including temperature, wind speed, and rainfall predictions, helping you plan your activities accordingly.

Zomato
Website: https://www.zomato.com/auckland
Description: Zomato is a popular app for discovering restaurants, cafes, and bars in Auckland. The app allows you to search for dining options based on location, cuisine, and price range, and features user reviews, ratings, and photos to help you make informed choices.

Culture Trip
Website: https://theculturetrip.com/pacific/new-zealand/auckland/
Description: Culture Trip is a travel app that offers curated recommendations for cultural experiences in Auckland. The app features articles and guides on local attractions, events, and activities, as well as insider tips from local writers and experts.

Wi-Fi Finder
Website: https://apps.apple.com/us/app/wi-fi-finder/id307217005
Description: Wi-Fi Finder is an app that helps you locate free Wi-Fi hotspots in Auckland and around the world. The app provides a map of nearby hotspots and allows you to filter results based on location, provider, and other criteria.

NZ Travel Guide
Website: https://www.newzealand.com/int/feature/new-zealand-travel-guide/
Description: NZ Travel Guide is a comprehensive app for planning and navigating your trip to New Zealand. The app offers information on accommodations, attractions, transportation, and more, with a focus on Auckland and other popular destinations.

First Aid by New Zealand Red Cross

Website: https://www.redcross.org.nz/first-aid/first-aid-app/
Description: The First Aid app by New Zealand Red Cross provides essential first aid information and advice, tailored to New Zealand conditions. The app features step-by-step instructions for various emergency situations, as well as a GPS-enabled hospital locator, making it a useful tool for travelers.

9.Eating in Auckland

Auckland is full of culinary surprises. The large migrant communities across the city have created a truly rich gastronomic culture and Aucklanders are very proud of the variety on offer in the city. Due to being a former colony, New Zealand cuisine itself is highly influenced by British cuisine, but there are a few twists that make it more distinct. Here are some typical Kiwi dishes worth trying:

- **Fish and Chips:** these are slightly different from the British variety and many visitors to both countries prefer the New Zealand style. The chips are fluffier in the middle and crispier on the outside, and the fish generally tastes fresher. New Zealanders typically have lashings of ketchup on their fish and chips, and there is not a vinegar bottle in sight. One thing to note is that Maori culture says it is disrespectful to eat seafood by the ocean, so most people eat these in the restaurants or take them to their home.
- **Meat Pies:** these are also a favorite in Australia, but Kiwis like to take meat pies to a new level by adding a layer of cheese sauce between the meat and pastry. As with most other dishes, it is customary to add lashings of ketchup on top before tucking in.
- **Pavlova:** there is a big debate between Australia and New Zealand about where this dish originated, but whilst in NZ you should just quietly nod when you are reassured it was, in fact, the kiwis that invented it. It is a large meringue filled with fruit and cream. Feijoas are a unique fruit to New Zealand, with a tart flavor, and will be commonly found within pavlovas across the country.
- **Kumara fries:** kumara is the Maori word for sweet potato, and the fries are almost always sold as an accompaniment in fast food joints. Rather than ketchup, these are generally served with garlic aioli. Though these are becoming increasingly more popular across the world, this dish has always been a staple to New Zealand cuisine and most places do them very well as a result.

- **Hangi:** if you attend a Maori cultural experience, you will likely be invited to join for a hangi. These are meals made in a pit in the ground with fire, and consist of meats, potatoes, and vegetables. It is a very unique way of preparing food, and no Maori cultural experience is complete without one. The rituals and etiquette surrounding this style of eating will be described to you before you commence, and it is highly advisable to pay attention to these.

Though these dishes are the most popular within New Zealand, Auckland, in particular, has a wide variety of foreign and fusion cuisines. We suggest you check out the following places to get a real taste of the different cultures that reside in the city:

- Dominion Road: often dubbed Auckland's Chinatown, locals fulfill their bizarre obsession with Chinese dumplings in this district. You can also get a wide range of other Asian cuisines in the area, and enjoy the impact the migrant community has made on the city. Outside of this area, there is also a great (and very cheap) Asian food court on Ponsonby Road.
- Silo Park: if you are visiting during the summer, this arts district is transformed into a food truck venue every Wednesday evening. Food truck culture is on the rise in New Zealand, and you will find many dotted around the city. Silo Park gathers a rotating selection of the most popular food trucks from across the city and accompanies the experience with live DJs and art installations.
- Wellesley Street, starting from Queen Street and heading west: this road features some of the best Latin American food in the city. Mexican and Chilean food is particularly popular thanks to the established migrant communities, but there are also some great Brazilian BBQ and Caribbean restaurants popping up. In particular, Mexican Café has become an Auckland institution and features a variety of cultural events as well as great tacos and ceviche.
- Newmarket: New Zealanders take their coffee culture seriously - like pavlova, they also argue that they invented and discovered the flat white

before Australians. Newmarket has some of the best-rated cafés in the city. These are very popular during brunch hours on weekends, and serve a variety of Kiwi and international fusion dishes. In Auckland, it is common to be asked how many shots of coffee you want in your flat white, but the standard elsewhere in New Zealand is a double shot. Ponsonby, Grey Lynn, and Takapuna also have great cafés.

- Central Auckland, Grafton, and Kingswell: burgers have exploded in popularity across the country since the 80s, and these three regions feature some of the best options. Burger Fuel is the main chain in Auckland and has some great gourmet offerings. The typical Kiwi burger consists of beetroot, egg, and aioli as toppings with a tonne of vegetables and a juicy burger. Inspired by Pacific Island cuisines, you will often find pineapple served as a topping option.

In general, New Zealanders try to go to restaurants with locally sourced ingredients whenever possible. There is a huge diversity of agriculture in the country and most menus will be seasonal. Avocados are particularly popular in the summer, however often face shortages in the winter which results in amusing wars between restaurants involving illegal avocado trades. In the winter, asparagus is also a common ingredient as well as beetroot and potatoes. The relative isolation the country faces from the rest of the world has resulted in a proud heritage of locally grown produce, and the wisest tourists follow suit to experience the best flavors the country has to offer.

Five Recommended Meals

Auckland is a foodie's paradise, with a variety of local cuisine that combines fresh ingredients and unique flavors. Here are five recommended meals with local cuisine that are sure to tantalize your taste buds:

1. **Appetizer: Tuatua Fritters**

Start your meal off with a local favorite - Tuatua Fritters. These crispy fritters are made with tuatua, a type of shellfish that is found in abundance in New

Zealand. They are served with a tangy lemon aioli and a side of fresh green

Main: Lamb Shank with Kumara Mash –
For the main course, try the classic Kiwi dish of Lamb Shank with Kumara Mash. This hearty dish features tender lamb shanks slow-cooked in red wine and herbs, served on top of creamy kumara (sweet potato) mash. It's a comfort food that will warm you up on any chilly evening.

Dessert: Pavlova - End your meal on a sweet note with the national dessert of New Zealand - Pavlova. This meringue-based dessert is crispy on the outside, soft and fluffy on the inside, and is topped with whipped cream and fresh fruit. It's light and refreshing, perfect for a summer evening.

Drink: Sauvignon Blanc - To accompany your meal, try a local wine like Sauvignon Blanc. New Zealand produces some of the world's best Sauvignon Blanc, with a crisp and refreshing taste that pairs well with seafood and other light dishes.

2.   **Appetizer: Whitebait Fritters** –
Another popular Kiwi appetizer is Whitebait Fritters. These small fish are mixed with egg and flour, then pan-fried until crispy. They are served with lemon wedges and a sprinkle of salt for a simple yet delicious taste.

Main: Hangi - For a taste of traditional Maori cuisine, try the Hangi. This method of cooking involves burying food in a pit in the ground with hot rocks and then steaming it for several hours. The result is tender and flavorful meat, vegetables, and potatoes that are infused with smoky flavor.

Dessert: Hokey Pokey Ice Cream - New Zealand's most beloved ice cream flavor is Hokey Pokey, which is made with vanilla ice cream and small pieces of honeycomb toffee. It's sweet and creamy, with a satisfying crunch.

Drink: Pinot Noir - Pinot Noir is a popular red wine in New Zealand, known for its fruity and earthy flavors. It pairs well with hearty dishes like the Hangi or other meats.

3.   **Appetizer: Paua Fritters** –

Paua is a type of abalone found in New Zealand's coastal waters. Paua Fritters are made by mixing paua with flour and egg, then deep-frying until golden brown. They are served with a sweet chili dipping sauce for a perfect combination of flavors.

Main: Fish and Chips - One of New Zealand's most famous dishes is Fish and Chips. Fresh, flaky fish is coated in crispy batter and served with thick-cut fries, tartar sauce, and lemon wedges. It's a classic Kiwi meal that is perfect for a casual dinner.

Dessert: Lolly Cake - For a unique dessert, try Lolly Cake. This treat is made by mixing crushed biscuits and colorful fruit-flavored candy (known as lollies) with condensed milk, then shaping it into a log and slicing it into pieces. It's a fun and playful dessert that kids and adults alike will love.

Drink: Craft Beer - New Zealand has a thriving craft beer scene, with many small breweries producing unique and flavorful brews. Try a local IPA or pale ale to complement your meal.

4. Appetizer : Mussels –

New Zealand is known for its fresh and delicious seafood, and Mussels are a must-try. These plump and juicy shellfish are steamed in a white wine and garlic sauce, then served with crusty bread to soak up all the flavorful juices.

Main: Hāngī Burger - For a modern twist on traditional Maori cuisine, try a Hāngī Burger. This burger features a juicy beef patty, topped with tender Hāngī-style pulled pork, caramelized onions, and a tangy BBQ sauce. It's served on a soft brioche bun with a side of crispy fries.

Dessert: Feijoa Crumble - Feijoa is a uniquely New Zealand fruit, with a tangy and slightly sweet flavor. Feijoa Crumble is a popular dessert that features this fruit, baked with a crispy crumble topping and served with a dollop of whipped cream. It's the perfect way to end your meal on a sweet note.

Drink: Kombucha - Kombucha is a fermented tea that has become popular in recent years for its health benefits. It's also a refreshing and delicious drink that pairs well with spicy or flavorful dishes.

5. Appetizer: Crayfish –

Crayfish (also known as rock lobster) is a delicacy in New Zealand, and a popular appetizer at many restaurants. The tender and sweet meat is served with a lemon and garlic butter sauce, or simply with a squeeze of lemon juice.

Main: Venison - New Zealand is home to some of the best venison in the world, with a rich and gamey flavor that pairs well with fruity or earthy sauces. Try a venison steak, served with a side of roasted vegetables and a red wine reduction sauce.

Dessert: Kiwifruit Cheesecake - Kiwifruit is another iconic New Zealand fruit, with a tangy and sweet flavor. Kiwifruit Cheesecake is a delicious dessert that combines creamy cheesecake with a tart kiwifruit topping. It's a refreshing and satisfying end to any meal.

Drink: Gin and Tonic - New Zealand has a thriving gin scene, with many small distilleries producing unique and flavorful gins. Try a local gin and tonic, garnished with a slice of cucumber or a sprig of rosemary, for a refreshing and herbaceous drink.

Vegan and vegetarian options

The Butcher's Son
Website: https://www.thebutchersson.co.nz/
Description: The Butcher's Son is a popular vegan eatery offering delicious plant-based versions of classic dishes, such as burgers, salads, and smoothie bowls. Their menu emphasizes locally sourced and organic ingredients, ensuring a flavorful and sustainable dining experience.

Little Bird Kitchen
Website: https://littlebirdorganics.co.nz/
Description: Little Bird Kitchen is a cozy cafe and restaurant specializing in raw, vegan, and gluten-free cuisine. Their menu features a variety of creative dishes, including raw pizzas, salads, and desserts, as well as cold-pressed juices and smoothies.

Lord of the Fries

Website: https://www.lordofthefries.co.nz/

Description: Lord of the Fries is a popular vegan fast-food chain offering a range of plant-based burgers, hot dogs, and fries. Their menu also includes a selection of vegetarian options, making it a convenient choice for a quick and satisfying meal.

Local food markets and street food

La Cigale French Market

Website: https://www.lacigale.co.nz/

Description: La Cigale French Market is a bustling food market held every weekend in Parnell. The market features a variety of local and imported food stalls, offering fresh produce, artisanal bread, pastries, cheeses, and more. Enjoy the lively atmosphere while sampling delicious street food and shopping for gourmet ingredients.

Matakana Village Farmers' Market

Website: https://www.matakanacountry.co.nz/market/

Description: Located just an hour north of Auckland, the Matakana Village Farmers' Market is a popular destination for food lovers. The market showcases the best of the region's local produce, including fresh fruits and vegetables, artisanal cheeses, and handmade chocolates. It's also a great opportunity to try some delicious street food and enjoy the surrounding village atmosphere.

Night Markets

Website: https://www.aucklandnightmarket.co.nz/

Description: Auckland's Night Markets are held in various locations throughout the week, offering a diverse selection of street food from around the world. Discover a variety of delicious dishes, from Malaysian roti to Japanese takoyaki, all while enjoying live music and entertainment.

Best cafes and coffee shops

Eighthirty Coffee Roasters
Website: https://eighthirty.com/
Description: Eighthirty Coffee Roasters is a popular cafe and coffee roastery in Auckland, offering expertly crafted coffee and a selection of light bites. With several locations throughout the city, Eighthirty is a great spot to enjoy a relaxing coffee break.

Bestie Café
Website: https://www.bestiecafe.com/
Description: Bestie Café is a charming cafe located in the heart of K'Road, offering a range of delicious breakfast and lunch dishes, as well as exceptional coffee. The cafe features a cozy interior and a sunny courtyard, making it a perfect spot for catching up with friends or enjoying some quiet time.

Remedy Coffee
Website: https://remedycoffee.business.site/
Description: Remedy Coffee is a hidden gem in Auckland's CBD, serving top-notch coffee and a selection of fresh, delicious pastries. The friendly staff and warm atmosphere make it an ideal spot for a quick caffeine fix or a leisurely catch-up.

Dietary considerations: gluten-free, halal, kosher, and more

The Midnight Baker
Website: https://www.themidnightbaker.co.nz/
Description: The Midnight Baker is a gluten-free and vegan-friendly cafe, offering a range of delicious breakfast and lunch dishes, as well as freshly baked goods. Their signature Freedom Loaf, a gluten-free and vegan bread, is a must-try for those with dietary restrictions.

Paradise Indian Food
Website: https://www.paradise-indian-food.co.nz/
Description: Paradise Indian Food offers a diverse menu of authentic Indian cuisine, with many vegetarian, vegan, and halal options available. The restaurant is known for its delicious curries and tandoori dishes, which can be customized to suit various dietary needs.

The Blue Rose Café
Website: https://www.thebluerose.co.nz/
Description: The Blue Rose Café is a cozy spot that offers a variety of dishes catering to dietary restrictions, including gluten-free, dairy-free, and vegetarian options. Their menu includes a mix of classic café fare and more adventurous dishes, ensuring there is something for everyone.

Taam
Website: http://taam.co.nz/
Description: Taam is a kosher bakery and café located in the suburb of Glenfield. They offer a range of kosher-certified products, including bread, pastries, and cakes, as well as a selection of savory dishes. With a focus on quality ingredients and traditional recipes, Taam is a great option for those seeking kosher dining options in Auckland.

Revive Vegetarian Café

Website: https://www.revive.co.nz/
Description: Revive Vegetarian Café is a popular healthy eatery with multip
locations in Auckland. Their menu focuses on fresh, wholesome ingredients
and includes a variety of vegetarian, vegan, and gluten-free options. Enjoy
delicious salads, hot pots, and wraps while adhering to your dietary
preferences.

10.Our 3-Day Travel Itinerary Suggestion

Day One

09:00 - Arrive at Auckland International Airport.
Due to stricter customs checks and passport control, the sheer size of the airport and the infamous Auckland traffic it can take some time to get from the plane to the city, so give yourself around two hours to do so. If you're arriving from elsewhere in New Zealand this will be much quicker as you will arrive at the domestic terminal and will not have to go through any of the checks

(https://pixabay.com/en/sky-city-tower-view-harbour-197768/)

11:00 - Once you have arrived in Auckland head straight towards the **Sky Tower**. Similar to other observation decks across the world, the Auckland Sky Tower has become a major symbol of the city since it was built in 1997. When you enter you can buy two different types of tickets - a single entry ticket or a "day and night" ticket. As we recommend you come back to SkyCity later, you can decide which ticket is best depending on your dining option in the evening - as some are located up the tower anyway. It can be worth your time making sure you get to see the view at both day and night for different perspectives of the city. Spend about an hour here taking photos and admiring views over the city and the Hauraki Gulf.

12:00 - From the Sky Tower walk towards the harbor front and check out the **New Zealand Maritime Museum**. This museum gives a great overview of the country's extensive seafaring culture as well as interactive exhibits about Maori ships, migration and old Kiwiana (the name given to symbols associated with the country). There's also a boat trip included in your ticket if the weather is good. It's a small museum, so with the boat trip factored in it should only take you an hour and a half.

13:30 - Continue walking along the harbourfront to **Wynyard Quarter** - Auckland's young and trendy district. Here you will find a number of restaurants and bars as well as Silo Park - an art exhibition space made out of disused storage silos and shipping containers. There's also a shipping container library, a futuristic park and great views over the harbor. For lunch, you have a few great options: Rushworth where you can sample typical casual New Zealand dining including sandwiches, egg dishes, and pies; Sal's which has become an Auckland institution for great New York style pizza; or Live Fish which serves up some of the finest New Zealand seafood with an Asian twist. Take your time here to explore the area and enjoy the food.

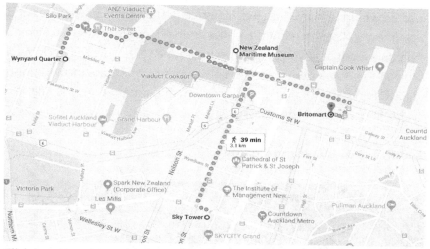

Click here to access the map through Google Maps

16:00 - Head back along the waterfront to **Britomart** and grab a train to either **Parnell** or **Grafton**. From here you can head to **Auckland Domain** - the largest park in the city. Here you have a selection of beautiful gardens, most featuring a variety of New Zealand native plant life and one in an Asian style. The walkways are lined with native trees that wind and twist above to make a natural archway. Auckland War Memorial Museum is also based here if you would like to visit. We recommend at least visiting the grounds of the museum but if you can you should enter to learn more about the ANZACs and the deep military history New Zealand shares with Australia. We suggest starting at the Grafton end of the park, heading towards the museum and then walking down to the winter gardens. From there you can then take the Lover's Walkthrough to the university district. The park is huge, and the museum will take at least an hour, so give yourself plenty of time to explore.

19:00 - The Universities end of the park is just a short walk away from SkyCity, so now it is time to head back. Whilst at SkyCity you can enjoy your dinner at one of the many restaurants on offer. We have included a guide below to everything available within the complex. Once you have had your dinner you can then enjoy the bars, entertainment offerings and casino located within SkyCity. This area is frequented by some of New Zealand's wealthiest so keep in mind the prices are high, but for a one-off visit it is definitely worth it. If you're lucky, you might also be able to check out a show at the Aotea Centre or Q Theatre, both of which are located right next to SkyCity. Take your time to enjoy your night, but prepare yourself for an action-packed the second day!

ZoomTip 1.1 - Auckland SkyCity

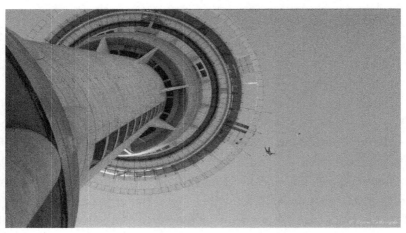

(link)

Auckland SkyCity was developed to accompany the Sky Tower and both were completed in 1997. This large entertainment complex features all walks of life from across the city, although only the wealthiest Kiwis can be seen there regularly. Here are some things you can check out whilst there

- **Federal Delicatessen** - This delicatessen is based off New York Jewish delis and provides much of the same fare - carefully cured meats, fountain sodas and even a range of cocktails. It has won numerous awards and has become a favorite for Aucklanders. The prices are more reasonable here and the cups of coffee are bottomless.
- **Orbit 360 Dining -** If you only opted for a single day ticket when visiting the SkyTower earlier, dining here will give you free entry to the

tower at night time however do keep in mind this requires you to book in advance. It rotates - completing a full rotation every hour - giving you amazing 360-degree views over the whole of Auckland. It offers kiwi inspired food using only seasonally sourced ingredients.

- **twentyone** - This luxury late night bar concept is based in the main SkyCity complex and features a rotating series of well-curated DJs, cocktails and even a casual food menu if you start feeling a little peckish. The bartenders are all very experienced and fully trained in flair bartending making the process of getting your cocktail a show in itself. The interiors have a very luxurious feel and this is a great place to drink the night away.
- **Casino** - Probably the most famous part of the SkyCity complex, this is the largest casino in New Zealand. There is live entertainment, a dedicated bar with snacks available and of course a huge array of casino games. There are over 150 table games and thousands of machines ready for you to chance your luck with. Do gamble responsibly, but there are plenty of events in this part of the complex to keep you entertained when you're away from the tables. There is a dress code - keep neat and tidy - and you must be 20 or over to enter the gaming area. You can, however, enter other areas without restriction.
- **Events** - Though most of the events are based in the casino complex, some are spread out across the restaurants and hotel. These include bingo, theatre, music performances, culinary workshops, and cultural experiences. To keep up to date with what is on whilst you are visiting, check out the events tab of the Auckland SkyCity website.

Day Two

09:00 - You should aim to arrive at the ferry terminal (next to Britomart) at about 9 am so you can catch the 09:25 sailing to **Rangitoto**. We've include a guide below to what you need and what you can do there, but taking the first boat there and the next available boat back to Auckland will leave you with plenty of time to explore the largest volcano in Auckland. Please keep in mind you should book the ferry online in advance from the Fullers Ferrie website.

Fullers360 is a ferry company that offers affordable and comfortable transportation services to Auckland's surrounding islands and tourist destinations. With a fleet of modern and well-equipped vessels, Fullers360 provides passengers with a relaxing and enjoyable travel experience.

One of the most popular routes is the trip to Waiheke Island, with ferry tickets starting at around $40 NZD per person for a return trip, and the journey taking approximately 40 minutes each way. Once on the island, visitors can explore the beaches, vineyards, and local attractions. The cost c activities on the island varies, but expect to pay around $20-$30 NZD for a wine tasting experience or a guided tour.

Fullers360 also offers regular ferry service to Rangitoto Island, with tickets starting at around $36 NZD per person for a return trip, and the journey taking approximately 25 minutes each way. Visitors can explore the island's volcanic cone and unique flora and fauna. The cost of hiking to the top of the cone is free, but visitors must book a guided tour for approximately $3(NZD per person.

To book ferry tickets with Fullers360, visitors can purchase tickets online through their website or at the downtown Auckland ferry terminal. It's recommended to book in advance, especially during peak travel periods, to ensure availability.

The website address for Fullers360 is https://www.fullers.co.nz/.

(https://www.flickr.com/photos/xiquinho/8150285930/in/album-
72157631917728814/)

13:15 - This is the time the boat will be due to arrive at the harbor. We suggest taking an hour to relax before preparing for the next activity. There's a small astroturfed area next to the boat terminal with seating and dining establishments including sushi, coffee, and health food. You can also check out the Cloud - a huge building right by the edge of the water with large indoor board games and table tennis tables which are free to use. Inside the terminal, you will also find **Island Gelato Company**, who sell surprisingly excellent gelato in a variety of flavors.

14:00 - No trip to New Zealand is complete without a **bungee jump** and **Auckland Harbour Bridge** is the best option for those who are new to the extreme sport. You will be picked up at the waterfront close to the ferry terminal and taken straight to the jump center attached to the bridge. AJ Hackett will then brief you, attach all the gear and walk you along the inside of the bridge to the jump site. You can opt for three types of jump - dry, touch or dunk - depending on how much water you want to be exposed to. They also provide a certificate at the end and you can opt to purchase photography and video footage. This needs to be booked online in advance at the AJ Hackett website. You can often get good deals on the prices of the jump on special days and during the low season. Our final piece of advice? Don't look down!

(https://pixabay.com/en/bungy-bungee-extreme-sports-184/)

17:00 - The bungee jump team will drop you off back at the city center again. From here we suggest walking down Queen Street and turning onto Victoria Street where you can have dinner at Mexican Café. This Mexican restaurant is famous with locals and visitors alike and showcases the best cuisine available from the Mexican expat community in Auckland. We recommend the ceviche starter, carnitas tacos and the chocolate cake for dessert. They also have the best margaritas in town - the perfect way to cool off and unwind after an action-packed a day in Auckland.

19:00 - You may want to call it an early one after a long day of sailing on the Hauraki, hiking around a volcano and jumping off a bridge, but if not you should definitely wander further up Queen Street until you end up at K Road. This is Auckland's Alternative street and will give you an interesting glimpse into the various counter-cultures found within the city. If you are interested in connecting with the local LGBTQ+ community, check out one of the many provocatively named bars along the strip (such as the Dog's Bollix or 69). Though the street is notorious for its strip clubs, drag shows, and sex shops, there are also some interesting alternative scenes to check out that involves none of these. **St Kevin's Arcade** has a few small bars serving whiskey, mulled wine and cigars. The Turkish community operates a string of restaurants across the strip and the baklava is to die for. If you like alternative electronic music, you should definitely check out Neck of the Woods - though they also provide a variety of other cultural events throughout the week. Though K Road once had a rough reputation, it has grown its own open and accepting community and even if you do not plan on visiting any of the establishments it is still interesting to have a look at how the road transforms during the evenings.

ZoomTip 2.1 – Rangitoto

Located in the Hauraki Gulf off the coast of the North Shore, Rangitoto Island is home to the largest volcano in the Auckland Volcanic Zone. Nevertheless, you should not worry as it has been over 500 years since the last eruption and it is expected to stay quiet for thousands more.
Visiting this island will give you a rewarding insight into the nature New Zealand has to offer and the impact volcanic activity has had on the North

Island. You have two options to get to the summit:

Hike - The most popular route is **the Summit Track** is this is the most well signposted. You will walk through lush volcanic forests and be rewarded with a breathtaking view over Auckland City when you reach the summit. There's also the opportunity to turn off part of the way through to check out the lava caves. If you are more adventurous, you can also try out the track that takes you to the adjoining island - Motutapu.

One of the most popular activities on the island is hiking the **Summit Track**, which offers stunning views of the island and surrounding Hauraki Gulf. Here's a guide to help you plan and enjoy your hike:

- Getting there: To get to Rangitoto Island, take a Fullers360 ferry from Auckland's downtown ferry terminal. Once on the island, follow signs to the Summit Track, which is located near the wharf.
- Road train - This is a four wheel drive vehicle that will carry you up the hill, and is a great option if you do not feel able to hike to the top. It is guided, and though it does not take you directly to the summit it does take you to a small boardwalk that you can cross to reach the top.
- Trail information: The Summit Track is approximately 2.4 km (1.5 miles) each way, with a steep ascent to the summit. The trail is well-maintained and marked, but can be rocky and uneven in some areas. The hike is considered moderately difficult, and takes approximately 1-2 hours to complete round-trip.
- What to bring: Be sure to wear sturdy walking shoes or hiking boots, as well as comfortable clothing for the weather conditions. Bring plenty of water and snacks, as there are no food or drink options along the trail. Sunscreen, a hat, and sunglasses are also recommended, as there is little shade on the trail.
- Summit views: The summit of Rangitoto offers stunning panoramic views of the island and surrounding Hauraki Gulf. Take time to enjoy the view and take some photos before heading back down the trail.
- Please keep in mind that there is nowhere on the island to get food or drink so take plenty of snacks and water with you. If you forget last

minute there is a shop on the ferry. The ferries are scheduled for the same times every day, so make sure not to miss yours or you will be stuck there. Always aim to get the earliest ferry to the island so even if you miss the next ferry back you will still likely make one of the 2-3 later ferries.

- A 7:30 am ferry runs only on Saturdays. Fullers offer discounts on these early bird tickets. The earliest ferry every other day is at 9:25 am.
- Other activities: If you have time, consider exploring some of the other attractions on Rangitoto Island, such as the lava caves or the beaches. There are also guided tours available, which provide additional insight and information about the island's unique geology and history.

Overall, hiking the Summit Track on Rangitoto Island is a must-do activity for visitors to Auckland. With stunning views and a moderate challenge, it's a great way to explore the natural beauty of this unique volcanic island.

Day Three

10:00 - Have a long rest after a long day and wake up a little later. From where you are staying you should head out to **Kohimarama Beach.** The Eastern Beaches are very popular with locals however **Mission Bay**, whilst the most well-known can get extremely busy. If you go a little further to **Kohimarama** you will find a much quieter beach with the same view of Rangitoto and warm summer waters. The beach is flanked with a rustic boardwalk and trees, giving it a much more idyllic and relaxed vibe than neighboring Mission Bay.

Whilst at Kohimarama, you can grab brunch at **Kohi Corner**. Owned by an award-winning Auckland company, this café is an example of a New Zealand coffee culture at its finest. An interesting and seasonal menu, combined with great barista coffee and weekend specials, give you the ultimate Kiwi brunch experience. We suggest you spend a good three hours at Kohimarama relaxing at the beach and enjoying brunch.

(link)

13:00 - From Kohimarama grab a bus to the Mount Eden neighborhood. Mount Eden is probably the most famous volcano in the city and gives excellent views over the CBD, Hauraki Gulf, and Sky Tower. It is an easy climb to the top and you will be greeted by many local joggers and dog walkers offering their encouragement. It should only take a couple of hours if you take a relaxed stroll and plan to explore a little at the top.

15:00 - For the final part of your trip it is time to head to Ponsonby Road for some shopping. We recommend starting at the College Hillside and walking towards K Road from there. Ponsonby Road is full of boutique style shops with local independent designers and craftspeople on display. There are also some brands, but almost all of them are either New Zealander or Australian. If you are hungry we suggest grabbing a bite to eat ahead of your flight at Ponsonby International Foodcourt. Most of the best food here is Asian -, particularly the Malaysian and Cambodian stands. If you would prefer some burgers you should instead check out Murder Burger. All of their burgers have a very kiwi twist and use seasonal ingredients. Ponsonby Road is a great place to get souvenirs to take home to friends and family. Both food and consumer goods are generally more expensive at the airport so this is a great option for last minute shopping and the gifts will likely be far more unique and representative of New Zealand.

18:00 - Once you have finished up at Ponsonby Road you can start walking down K Road where there is an airport bus stop. This is only used some parts of the day, so a safer option might be Queen Street which is joined on to K Road. Keep in mind the terrible traffic could mean it could take you over an hour to get to the airport, so factor that in when deciding what exact time to leave. For domestic flights to elsewhere in New Zealand you only have to check in 50 minutes early, but for international flights, this is generally 2-3 hours depending on the airline.

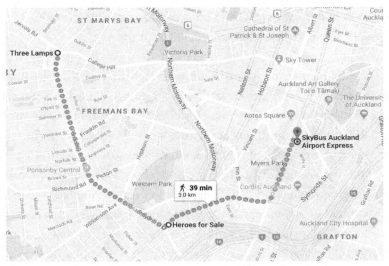

[Click here to access the map through Google Maps](#)

Place	Website Address	GPS Location
Kohimarama Beach	https://www.aucklandnz.com/visit/discover/nature/beaches/kohimarama-beach	-36.8709, 174.8535
Kohi Corner	https://www.kohi.co.nz/	-36.8754, 174.8534
Mount Eden	https://www.aucklandnz.com/visit/discover/nature/volcanoes/mount-eden	-36.8797, 174.7648
Ponsonby Road	https://www.aucklandnz.com/visit/discover/arts-culture-history/shopping-ponsonby-road	-36.8525, 174.7445
Ponsonby International Foodcourt	https://www.facebook.com/PonsonbyInternationalFoodcourt/	-36.8505, 174.7449
Murder Burger	https://www.murderburger.co.nz/	-36.8495, 174.7435
Auckland Airport	https://www.aucklandairport.co.nz/	-37.0082, 174.7850

ZoomTip 3.1 - New Zealand Coffee Culture

Both New Zealand and Australia take great pride in their coffee culture, and there is some debate as to who actually invented the flat white. While opinions may differ, many New Zealanders will proudly claim that their version of this popular coffee beverage is the best. When visiting a coffee shop in New Zealand, it's worth knowing a few key details about coffee etiquette and the unique styles of coffee available.

Generally, espressos (known locally as short blacks), macchiatos, and cappuccinos are similar to those found in other parts of the world, but the milk in New Zealand is typically much more textured and velvety. Flat whites, which are served in smaller cups, have a larger ratio of coffee to milk, making them stronger. This is the drink where textured milk was first experimented with, and in Auckland, you may be asked if you want one or two shots of coffee, while elsewhere in the country, you will be given two shots automatically. Lattes are made like flat whites but in glasses that hold more milk, making them weaker. These are the two most popular coffee drinks in the country.

Long blacks, similar to Americanos, are also stronger in New Zealand than elsewhere in the world. In Auckland, it's common to be given the espresso and hot water in separate vessels so you can adjust the strength of your coffee to your liking. Piccolos are smaller than flat whites but larger than macchiatos and contain the same type of milk as flat whites. These are generally consumed quickly by people on the go, but they are also a good option if you prefer your coffee strong.

When you visit a café or coffee shop in New Zealand, you'll typically be seated by a member of staff and given menus. After finishing your meal or beverage, you'll be expected to pay at the till. This can be confusing for some foreign visitors who are used to paying at the table, but it's important to note that many local workers prefer customers to pay at the till, as their systems may not be set up for table payments. If you're simply grabbing a coffee to go, just let the staff member know and they will point you to the till.

While tipping is not expected in New Zealand, it is considered polite to leave a dollar or two in the tip jar if you enjoyed your coffee. Tips are usually split among all of the staff, including kitchen staff, rather than kept solely by the server. Because wages are generally high in New Zealand, workers do not rely heavily on tips to supplement their incomes.

Useful Phrases

Though English is the most widely spoken language, there are a few quirks to New Zealand English compared to other forms of the language that you should be aware of. Please be aware that New Zealanders slide their vowels - so ih sounds like uh and eh sounds like ih. This has been parodied with tongue in cheek adverts for deck washers and can sometimes make visitors double take.

In general, language differences fall into two categories - Maori influence on the language, and local slang terms that have become part of New Zealand English.

Everyday Maori Terms
Aotearoa - New Zealand
Aroha - love
Hangi - traditional Maori meal
Haka - Maori war dance, popular with rugby fans
Hui - local meeting
Iwi - translates literally as tribe, can be used to mean any close group of people such as families or friend groups
Kai - food
Karakia - prayer
Kia ora - greeting (often used instead of hello)
Koha - gift or donation
Korero - speak (both as a verb and noun)
Mana - reputation/power
Marae - a traditional Maori meeting house

Pakeha - Maori word for New Zealanders of European descent

Pounamu - translates as jade, but most Maori style pendants are now called pounamu

Puku - stomach

Taane/Tane - male (some toilets use this)

Taonga - precious items

Te reo - language

Wahine - female (some toilets use this)

Waiata - song

Waka - translates literally as the canoe Maori traditionally used, but now can refer to any transport vessel

Whanau - family

Whare - house/home

Whare paku - toilet

Whenua - land/homeland/country

Common slang

Bach - a holiday home

Barbie - BBQ

Chilly bin - cooler box

Churrs - Cheers/Thank you

Dairy - Convenience store

Gumboots - Wellington Boots

Heaps - A lot

Jandals - flip flops

Mean - cool/great (i.e. "that pie was mean" means it was a great pie)

Sweet as - cool/OK/all good

No worries/no wurrs - no problem

Satched - wet

She'll be right - everything will be fine

Togs - swimming shorts

Tramping - hiking

Ute - pick-up truck

Across the ditch - Across the sea, in reference to Australia

Chips - these refer to both fries and chips/crisps in New Zealand. Sometime distinction is made with fries being referred to as hot chips, but often it isn' so careful when ordering food and ask if you are unsure.

Eh - used for reinforcement, similar to stereotypical Canadian usage.

Stubbies - cans of beer/very short men's shorts

Yeah, nah - No

Nah, yeah - Yes

Wop-wops - middle of nowhere

Thank you

Auckland is a vibrant and exciting city, with a range of activities, attractions, and cultural experiences to enjoy. From exploring the city's museums and galleries, to sampling its delicious food and wine, to taking in the natural beauty of its surrounding islands and coastline, Auckland has something to offer for everyone.

By following the practical tips and information provided in this guide, visitors can make the most of their time in Auckland and ensure a memorable and enjoyable trip. From planning your accommodation and transportation, to discovering the city's top tourist attractions and cultural experiences, to venturing out on day trips to nearby destinations, Auckland offers endless opportunities for adventure and discovery.

We hope this guide has been helpful in planning your trip to Auckland, and that you have a wonderful time exploring all that this beautiful city has to offer. Safe travels!

Have an amazing time in Aotearoa!

Your friends at Guidora.

Copyright Notice

Note to other copyright owners

We are grateful to those copyright owners who have given permission for their material to be used. Some of the material comes from secondary and tertiary sources. In every case, we have tried to locate the original author or photographer and make the appropriate acknowledgment. In some cases, the sources have proved obscure, and we have been unable to track them down. In these cases, we would like to hear from the copyright owners and will be pleased to acknowledge them in future editions or remove the material.

Made in the USA
Las Vegas, NV
20 January 2024